NEW LIBRARY

Volume V

NEW LIBRARY

A TRIBUTE TO THE ERUDITION OF CONSTANTINE CAVARNOS

Reviews of Forty-Two of His Books on Patristics, Philosophy, Hellenism, Spiritual Life, Modern Orthodox Saints, Ecumenism, and the Ecclesiastical Arts

VOLUME FIVE

by
Archbishop Chrysostomos of Etna

INSTITUTE FOR BYZANTINE
AND MODERN GREEK STUDIES
115 Gilbert Road
Belmont, Massachusetts 02478-2200
U.S.A.

Published by THE INSTITUTE FOR BYZANTINE
AND MODERN GREEK STUDIES, INC.
115 Gilbert Road
Belmont, Massachusetts 02478-2200

Library of Congress Control Number: 89-80265

Printed in the United States of America

ISBN 978-1-884729-90-4

CONTENTS

Contents

INTRODUCTION

By
Archbishop Chrysostomos
Center for Traditionalist Orthodox Studies

It was with great pleasure that I accepted the invitation of Professor Constantine Cavarnos and his learned associate, the Reverend Father Dr. Asterios Gerostergios, on behalf of the Institute for Byzantine and Modern Greek Studies, to author the fifth volume in the popular series *New Library*. This acclaimed series of critical reviews and evaluations of books in the fields of ancient, Byzantine, and modern Greek studies, Russian thought, and Eastern Orthodox spirituality, initiated by Dr. Cavarnos, was inspired by the famous *Bibliotheke* (*Library*) or *Myriobiblion* of the ninth-century Orthodox luminary, St. Photios the Great, to whom many attribute the "invention" of the book review. The extensive analyses and reviews of the several hundred books found in the Saint's *Library* constitute an encyclopedic feat widely praised by the *literati* of his day. *New Library* has earned similar accolades from contemporary research experts in the fields which it covers.

The previous four volumes of *New Library* appeared in 1989, 1992, 1995, and 2002, respectively. Volumes I, II, and IV were compilations of book reviews by Professor Cavarnos, while Volume III was written by his gifted brother, the late Dr. John P. Cavarnos, a classicist, Byzantinist, and historian, on books concerning classical Greek culture, the Church Fathers, medieval and modern Greek poetry, and the Orthodox Church. As I noted above, these volumes have been *enthusiastically received* and *positively reviewed* by a number of distinguished scholars in diverse areas of study.

The present volume of *New Library* is dedicated to reviews of a large number of works by Professor Cavarnos, an astonishingly prolific writer. These reviews were published, in most instances, in *Orthodox Tradition,* the journal of the Center for Traditionalist Orthodox Studies (CTOS), in Etna, California, but also in *The Greek Orthodox Theological Review, The Hellenic Voice,* and *The Hellenic Chronicle,* between 1984 and 2009. The majority of the reviews (several in

Greek *and* English versions) are mine. However, I have also included commentaries by others at the CTOS: Bishop Auxentios of Photiki, Director of the Center; Archimandrite Akakios, its Associate Director; Hieromonk Patapios, Academic Director; and Hieromonk Gregory and Father James Thornton, both Research Associates on the staff of the Center.

The reader will note that my reviews in this book have been left with my signature as it was when they were published. Thus, they are signed "Archimandrite Chrysostomos," "Bishop Chrysostomos" (of Oreoi *or* of Etna), my former titles, and "Archbishop Chrysostomos" (of Etna), my present title. Similarly, Bishop Auxentios' reviews are designated by his present title and by his former titles, "Hieromonk Auxentios" or "Archimandrite Auxentios." Reviews by Hieromonk Patapios, who wrote for *Orthodox Tradition* before entering the monastic life, also appear under his religious name and his secular name, "Patrick G. Barker."

Sunday of the Samaritan Woman
May 4/17, 2009

ALPHABETICAL LIST OF BOOKS
REVIEWED AND SOURCES OF REVIEWS

1. *The Anti-Papist Writings of Photios Kontoglou.* In *Orthodox Tradition*, Vol. XI, No. 3 (1994), pp. 43-44. (Originally appeared in *The Hellenic Voice,* in Greek.)

2. *Aristotle's Theory of the Fine Arts.* In *Orthodox Tradition*, Vol. XIX, Nos. 3-4 (2002), pp. 40-41.

3. *Biological Evolutionism.* In *Orthodox Tradition*, Vol. XII, No. 3 (1995), pp. 54-56.

4. *Blessed Elder Gabriel Dionysiatis.* In *Orthodox Tradition*, Vol. XVII, Nos. 2-3 (2000), pp. 56-57.

5. *Blessed Elder Iakovos of Epiros, Elder Joseph the Hesychast, and Mother Stavritsa the Missionary.* In *Orthodox Tradition*, Vol. XVIII, No. 4 (2001), pp. 37-38.

6. *Blessed Elder Philotheos Zervakos.* In *Orthodox Tradition*, Vol. XI, No. 3 (1994), pp. 45-47.

7. *Byzantine Chant.* In *Orthodox Tradition*, Vol. XVI, No. 2 (1999), p. 31.

8. *Byzantine Church Architecture.* In *Orthodox Tradition*, Vol. XXV, No. 2 (2008), pp. 23-24.

9. *Byzantine Churches of Thessaloniki.* In *Orthodox Tradition*, Vol. XIII, No. 1 (1996), pp. 65-66.

10. *The Concept of Christian Love.* In *Orthodox Tradition*, Vol. XIII, No. 2 (1996), pp. 59-60.

11. *Cultural and Educational Continuity of Greece.* In *Orthodox Tradition*, Vol. XII, No. 4 (1995), pp. 53-54.

12. *Ecumenism Examined.* In *Orthodox Tradition*, Vol. XIV, Nos. 2-3 (1997), p. 73.

13. *The Educational Philosophy of Benjamin of Lesvos.* In *The Greek Orthodox Theological Review*, Vol. XXXIII, No. 1 (Spring 1988), pp. 115-116.

14. *Fasting and Science.* In *Orthodox Tradition*, Vol. VI, No. 3 (1989), p. 6.

Alphabetical List of Books Reviewed

15. *Fine Arts and Tradition.* In *Orthodox Tradition*, Vol. XXII, No. 1 (2005), p. 46.

16. *The Future Life According to Orthodox Teaching.* In *Orthodox Tradition*, Vol. I, No. 2 (1984), pp. 46-47.

17. *Greek Letters and Orthodoxy.* In *Orthodox Tradition*, Vol. XXI, No. 2 (2004), pp. 40-41.

18. *Guide to Byzantine Iconography*: Volume Two. In *Orthodox Tradition*, Vol. XIX, Nos. 3-4 (2002), pp. 37-38.

19. *The Hellenic Heritage.* In *Orthodox Tradition*, Vol. XVII, Nos. 2-3 (2000), pp. 70-71.

20. *The Hellenic-Christian Philosophical Tradition.* In *Orthodox Tradition*, Vol. VII, No. 2 (1990), p. 10.

21. *Holiness: Man's Supreme Destiny.* In *Orthodox Tradition*, Vol. XIX, Nos. 3-4 (2002), pp. 38-39.

22. *Immortality of the Soul.* In *Orthodox Tradition*, Vol. XI, No. 1 (1994), p. 56.

23. *Man's Spiritual Evolution.* In *Orthodox Tradition*, Vol. XXIV, No. 3 (2007), pp. 65-66.

24. *Meetings with Kontoglou.* In *The Greek Orthodox Theological Review*, Vol. XXXII, No. 4 (Winter 1987), pp. 436-438; also in *Orthodox Tradition*, Vol. XI, No. 1 (1994), pp. 50-51.

25. *New Library,* Volume One. In *Orthodox Tradition*, Vol. VII, No. 2 (1990), p. 10.

26. *New Library,* Volume Two. In *Orthodox Tradition*, Vol. X, No. 1 (1993), pp. 44-46. (Originally appeared in *The Hellenic Chronicle.*)

27. *New Library,* Volume Four. In *Orthodox Tradition*, Vol. XXVI, No. 3 (2009), pp. 46-49.

28. *Orthodox Christian Terminology.* In *Orthodox Tradition*, Vol. XII, No. 1 (1995), p. 58.

29. *Orthodox Tradition and the Modern World.* In *Orthodox Tradition*, Vol. II, No. 2 (1985), pp. 10-11.

30. *Orthodoxy and Philosophy.* In *Orthodox Tradition*, Vol. XXI, No. 1 (2004), pp. 46-47.

Alphabetical List of Books Reviewed

39. St. Methodia of Kimolos. In *The Greek Orthodox Theological Review*, Vol. XXXII, No. 3 (Fall 1987), pp. 322-323.

40. St. Photios the Great. In *Orthodox Tradition*, Vol. XVI, No. 2 (1999), pp. 31-32.

41. St. Savvas the New. In *The Greek Orthodox Theological Review*, Vol. XXXI, Nos. 3-4 (Fall-Winter 1986), pp. 449-451.

42. Victories of Orthodoxy. In *Orthodox Tradition*, Vol. XV, Nos. 2-3 (1998), pp. 63-64.

I

REVIEWS OF *NEW LIBRARY*

1. *NEW LIBRARY*, VOLUME ONE

New Library, Volume One. Belmont, MA: Institute for Byzantine and Modern Greek Studies, 1989. Pp. 164 + Index.

This book contains reviews and discussions by Professor Cavarnos of various books—including Bishop (then Archimandrite) Chrysostomos' first volume of translations from the Desert Fathers (Hellenic College Press, 1980)—of interest to the philosopher, classicist, and student of Greek letters and Eastern Orthodox Christianity. Inspired by a similar work by St. Photios, this book, along with two anticipated volumes, will prove an especially precious guide to those wishing to gain an enlightened Orthodox view of a number of contemporary scholarly and literary works.

ARCHIMANDRITE AUXENTIOS
Center for Traditionalist
Orthodox Studies

2. *NEW LIBRARY*, VOLUME TWO

New Library, Volume Two. Belmont, MA: Institute for Byzantine and Modern Greek Studies, 1992. Pp. 198 + Index.

The first volume of *New Library*, comprised of reviews and summaries by Professor Cavarnos of books by or about Byzantine and modern Greek, as well as other, writers on philosophy, literary issues, and the Christian religion (particularly the Orthodox Faith), was published in 1989. The present volume consists of similar texts by Cavarnos, all of them written since 1989, and many of them taken from *The Hellenic Chronicle,* a Boston weekly.

The various chapters in this volume provide the reader with a vivid panorama of scholarship in all of the fields which I have mentioned above. The first chapter is a brilliant analysis of the responses of Nicholas Berdyaev, the provocative—if not always Orthodox—Russian social critic, to secular trends in Western scholarship, and especially the philosophy of Nihilism, or the rejection of God and spiritual precepts. The remaining chapters center on the writings of Orthodox thinkers, both Greek and Russian, who have refined Berdyaev's responses to Western secularization by a careful exposition of the teachings of the Orthodox Church and the philosophical, literary, and spiritual heritage which these teachings have bequeathed to Greek culture and to the cultures of Russia and the Slavic East.

As I noted in my own review of the first volume in this series, books of this kind are badly needed. First, at a time when even the educated read less and less, we need analytical apparatus to help us select good reading and to help us put that reading in context. Dr. Cavarnos' *New Library* does just this, by providing the reader with summaries and critical reviews of a large number of books (more than thirty in the present volume) in what is essentially a "programmed" course of development, guiding one from a clear statement of the problems of Western secular society to the solutions of these problems that Orthodox thinkers have drawn from the Hellenic-Christian traditions of Byzantine thought and Orthodox theology.

Second, Orthodox Christians, specifically, lack a clear understanding of their Faith. As an Orthodox traditionalist adhering to the Old Calendar, I can without hesitation say that even issues of acute theological and spiritual import are today "politicized" and made vulgar. "Correct words" have replaced correct thought, and the "correct line" has come to replace the primacy of personal conscience. Thus, resistance, dissent, and struggle—the very earmarks of Orthodox *unity*—have come to separate us Orthodox from one another. Our essential unity has been sacrificed for the pursuit of unity with the heterodox, of unity with the secular ethos of modern times or a humanistic vision of political and social unity. Ecumenism and its "branch theory" of the Church have rendered everything "equal," so that the unity that comes from a struggle for the prime truth—the product of a dialectical process of debate, exchange, and the refinement of our understanding of truth—is lost to us.

The essays in this volume address the need for Orthodox Christians to understand that the truth is in itself one, but that in its expressions

it is multi-faceted, rising as much out of spiritual anecdotes and theology as out of philosophy and literature. From the pages of this book,
we learn that the Orthodox claim to primacy, to
truth itself, is not an empty one, but one which
has drawn on many aspects of the truth, re-
flecting, in the unity of Orthodox thought, pro-
cesses of development, synthesis, and distilla-
tion that encompass Western secular thought
and reduce it to intellectual ash. Dr. Cavarnos
has brilliantly shown us that debate with, and
reaction to, secular thought, even in the context of disputes within Orthodoxy itself, have
created an intellectual hegemony that captures,
embodies, and properly reflects the wholeness
of Orthodox thought—a wholeness which is
not equal to *any other thing,* since it transcends
not only its component parts, finding unity in
diversity, but the very stuff of Western secular
thought and the sometimes superficial theological preoccupations which derive from it.

I consider the two current volumes of *New
Library* the first steps in what I believe will
prove to be a programmed text of Orthodox
education—an encyclopedia of thought drawn

from a critical synthesis of a wide range of writings from the Orthodox world. If this series is a crucial undertaking for Orthodox Christians, it constitutes a challenging and important treasury for Western thinkers, who will find in it evidence of the inequality of schools of thought and of the exalted primacy of Orthodox thought and the realms of intellectual pursuit which it has influenced.

As usual, this book, like the other publications of the Institute for Byzantine and Modern Greek Studies, is handsomely printed in a very durable paperback edition. It is a book which should be bought, read, treasured, and digested by all.

Bishop Chrysostomos
Center for Traditionalist
Orthodox Studies
[This review was reprinted
from *The Hellenic Chronicle*.]

3. *NEW LIBRARY*, VOLUME FOUR

Messages from the Holy Mountain. Volume IV in *New Library.* Belmont, MA: Institute for Byzantine and Modern Greek Studies, 2002. Pp. 133 + Indices and Bibliographical Notes.

Professor Constantine Cavarnos, that preëminent man of Orthodox letters, has compiled, in a new and superb volume of his *New Library,* critical commentaries on twenty recent works (published between 1951 and 2000) by various Fathers on the Holy Mountain of Athos. *New Library* is a series published by the Institute for Byzantine and Modern Greek Studies (IBMGS) and inspired by St. Photios the Great, the purported "father of the book review," and his work of similar title, *Bibliotheke,* or *Library.* This is the fourth of five volumes in the series to date, the present and the first and second volumes (1989 and 1992) written by Dr. Cavarnos; the third volume (1995) by his brother, the late Professor John P. Cavarnos; and a fifth volume (in press as of this writing and scheduled for release shortly by the IBMGS) written by me. Volume V features, primarily, my reviews (composed in Greek and English) of numerous books by Constantine Cavarnos, but also several reviews of his works by Bishop Auxentios of Photiki, Archimandrite Akakios Agiogregorites, Hieromonk Patapios Agiogregorites, Father James Thornton, and Hieromonk Gregory Agiogregorites, all published between 1984 and 2009 in *The Greek Orthodox Theological Review, Orthodox Tradition*, *The Hellenic Voice,* and *The Hellenic Chronicle.*

As the author notes in his Preface to this volume, it is in many ways a sequel to his two well-known and popular works on the Holy Mountain, *Anchored in God* and *The Holy Mountain,* as well as his celebrated fifteen-volume series, *Modern Orthodox Saints,* since some of the constituent volumes of this latter work are dedicated to, and cite a number of, Athonite Saints and holy personages. At the same time, as a volume of *New Library,* it is a sequel to a series of evaluative book reviews and scholarly commentaries that have thus far enjoyed significant attention from Orthodox ecclesiastical and theological authorities and from scholars in the fields of ancient Greek thought, modern Greek studies, Byzantine studies, and even Russian thought, given that the series treats with materials from all of these areas. Indeed, as Professor Cavarnos quite rightly observes—again in his Preface to the present work—"*New Library* is coming to be viewed as a kind of English-language encyclopedia in these fields." Harvard-educated, two times a Fulbright Scholar, and having enjoyed a distinguished teaching career at Harvard, the University of North Carolina, Clark University, Hellenic College, and other American institutions of higher learning, Dr. Cavarnos is a treasure; and his books, as one of the editors who sponsored the translation and publication of several of his works by the Patriarchal press of the Orthodox Church of Romania has remarked, are themselves a virtual compendium of Orthodox theological thought and Byzantine studies.

The twenty books, by a dozen authors and editors, reviewed by Dr. Cavarnos in the fourth volume of *New Library* afford one a rather expansive and rare insight into the spiritual work, theological thinking, and scholarly activities of some outstanding intellectual and spiritual figures on the Holy Mountain during the last seven decades of its thousand-year history. Let me make reference to some of this material, though by no means intending, thereby, to provide a *full profile* of the ideas and notions presented in this fascinating survey. One writer, portraying the traditional spiritual life of the Athonite monks in a general way, tells us that obedience, non-acquisitiveness, and a life of chastity and asceticism lie at the core of the monastic life. He rejects the idea that mere social service, as some believe, reflects the life of the Gospels. In another place, we are told that monastic life does not accommodate the life of the scholar or intellectual, but that the monk "lives" his spirituality; thus, the expositions and writings of genuine monastics condense and summarize the spiritual life. They do not approach learning with the desire to satisfy or enhance their egos, as secular scholars so often do, but from the spirit (as was the case with the great Hagiorite writer, St. Nicodemos), seeking to benefit themselves and others in a spiritual way.

Another chapter covers a work that criticizes autonomous humanism, which places man, and not God, at the center of life, leading to spiritual and social catastrophe and the eventual dissolution of the human person. One of the monks from among those whose works are cited anonymously wrote an introduction to the English translation of the *Philokalia.* He candidly opines that most Orthodox today live at a low spiritual level and are not capable of understanding the spiritual philosophy of the "university" of the *Philokalia.* He advises Orthodox to start their reading with the "spiritual elementary school" of the Lives of the Saints and then to move on to the "high school" of the *Evergetinos* (the writings of the Desert Fathers)— counsel which Dr. Cavarnos has for many years repeated. In another chapter, we are told of a book that has as its theme the great holiness which has characterized monastic life on Athos over the centuries. Yet another work speaks of the excellent library and learned outlook of a certain Athonite author who, for all that, inexorably brought his reading and erudition into the service of spiritual transformation.

The volume also includes reviews of books that speak to the phenomenon of miracles in the personal lives and witness of holy individuals from our own days and of works that recount

11

miraculous occurrences involving some of the Holy Mountain's famous Icons. Another book addresses the distortion of the Patristic witness in modern Orthodox writers, often educated in, and influenced by, the West, who seek to speak of liberation theology, a theology of eroticism, or a theology of external "joy" — of "theologies" that draw one away from the other-worldliness and sobriety of Orthodox spiritual pursuits. Very enlightening reference is likewise made to the rôle of the "university of the desert" (the monastery) in educating and forming a harmony in man through fine arts — music, poetry, and painting — in a context where the Church is at the center of one's experience, aims, goals, and self-understanding.

These themes, as I said, are but a sampling of the many topics and spiritual principles that are discussed in the books which Professor Cavarnos reviews and evaluates. Each piece forms part of the mosaic that emerges from his total presentation, which clearly and eloquently paints a portrait of the Holy Mountain, of the monastic life, and of many of the spiritual precepts that constitute Orthodoxy in its authentic and enduring expression. In the encyclopedia of *New Library*, this "entry" under monasticism is yet another wonderful contribution to our general understanding of Orthodoxy, its spiritual life, and the historical, philosophical, and intellectual worlds from which Orthodox Christianity emerged and which it has helped transform through the power of Divine wisdom.

This volume is one which I recommend to the Orthodox and non-Orthodox reader alike, as well as to scholarly specialists and the interested everyday reader. It is written in clear, understandable language and is adorned with numerous useful apparatus, including an index of subjects, an index of proper names, and a handy listing of the contents of the previous volumes (I-III) of *New Library*.

ARCHBISHOP CHRYSOSTOMOS
Center for Traditionalist
Orthodox Studies

II

TERMINOLOGY

1. *ORTHODOX CHRISTIAN TERMINOLOGY*

Orthodox Christian Terminology. Belmont, MA: Institute for Byzantine and Modern Greek Studies, 1994. Pp. 80.

English-speaking Orthodox have for decades tried to establish a standard nomenclature for speaking about their Church, its services, and its customs. Unfortunately, most efforts have resulted in the adoption of Roman Catholic and Protestant terms, which misrepresent the uniqueness of our Faith, or the use of such exotic stupidities as "writing" (i.e., "painting") Icons or "latrevizing" (i.e., "worshipping") in "Temples" ("Churches"), which represent eccentric translations of original Greek ecclesiastical terms. In the present superb book, Professor Cavarnos gives us a reasonable set of guidelines in establishing a consistent terminology that avoids these extremes.

Terminology

In his work on the English text of the Greek *Philokalia*, Dr. Cavarnos established a trend towards the de-Latinization of Greek names (e.g., "Demetrios" for "Demetrius"). In this new book, he suggests perpetuating this trend, though he wisely grants that one should use the standard English forms of names, when they exist. Thus, one need not write "Antonios" or "Antony" for "Anthony" or "Kyprianos" for "Cyprian." While I prefer descriptive appellations in their original, and thus speak of St. John Chrysostomos (not "Chrysostom") in English, Dr. Cavarnos is quite right in pointing out that the "Hellenization" of Greek names with clear English counterparts (e.g., "St. Ioannis Chrysostomos") can be unduly obscure.

Dr. Cavarnos also points out that the Orthodox Church employs poetic diction in its services and that the use of the English "You," instead of "Thou," in referring to God in liturgical worship is inconsistent with such diction. He likewise makes a very compelling argument for the theological unacceptability of Orthodox liturgical texts in English which avoid the distinction between "Thou" and "You" that one finds in the original Greek and Slavonic texts of the Liturgy.

The book goes on to consider the proper names for Icons (e.g., the "Touching," not "Unbelief," of St. Thomas), for Church services, for parts of the Church building, and for the various musical traditions of the Church (e.g., "Mode" for "Tone"). Dr. Cavarnos' guidelines are excellent and precise. Lovers of the exotic and obscurantists will not like them; scholars will. Every English-speaking Orthodox writer and believer should have this book next to his dictionary.

Bishop Chrysostomos

Center for Traditionalist
Orthodox Studies

2. *PHILOSOPHICAL DICTIONARY*

Philosophical Dictionary: English-Greek and Greek-English. Belmont, MA: Institute for Byzantine and Modern Greek Studies, 2006. Pp. 261.

Terminology

This is one of several books by Professor Cavarnos recently published by the Institute for Byzantine and Modern Greek Studies. It is an indispensable and truly recherché reference work—something that has certainly been as long needed as it has been sorely missed. Its purpose is to provide, as the subtitle to the volume tells us, a precise and erudite guide to the translation and use of Greek terminology in the areas of philosophy, Classics, modern Greek studies, theology, and the humanities in general. This is a wonderful companion work to Dr. Cavarnos' earlier volume, *Orthodox Christian Terminology* (Belmont, MA: Institute for Byzantine and Modern Greek Studies, 1994), a Greek-English and English-Greek glossary of Orthodox theological, liturgical, and general ecclesiastical terms that has for over a decade enjoyed much popularity among students of theology, ecclesiastical art and architecture, and hagiology. Like its earlier counterpart, the present dictionary is diglot, making it a superb resource for students, scholars, and researchers who work in both English and Greek.

The ultimate purpose of Professor Cavarnos' *Philosophical Dictionary* is precisely that of his earlier dictionary of Greek religious terms used in the Orthodox Church: to produce a standardized English-language vocabulary which accurately and precisely defines the specific fields of inquiry covered in this new reference work. In fact, the earlier *Orthodox Christian Terminology* is introduced by an excellent and informative essay that carefully describes this goal (see pp. 9-21). I must confess that in my own writing and translations, falling back, as I often do, on conventions of my own (some admittedly idiosyncratic, others reasonably considered), I too often stray from the specific guidelines set forth by Dr. Cavarnos—guidelines established during his long and distinguished academic career and associations with some of the finest scholars in the areas of study to which this newer book and his older publication are addressed. When I do stray in this way, it is ineluctably *to my personal detriment* and in inevitable disservice to the punctilious scholarship which Cavarnos embodies and to

18

which he calls the academic community in all of his publications.

I hope that others will follow me in adopting the conventions and suggestions made in this unique reference work, *Philosophical Dictionary*, which is very handsomely produced and beautifully bound. As is always the case when reviewing his refulgent works, I want to express, here, my unreserved and enthusiastic endorsement of Dr. Cavarnos' present reference book. He is one of the *more important Byzantinists and Orthodox religious writers of the twentieth and twenty-first centuries;* and his numerous writings are, to be sure, a guiding light to those of us who wish to preserve the precious tradition of *clarity* and *precision* in expressing the classical Hellenic heritage and the Eastern Orthodox tradition—the latter, in its earliest expression, and in part still today, a product of the Hellenic world—in the English language.

I should note that the fascinating and enjoyable Preface to *Philosophical Dictionary* (pp. 5-18) contains an account of Professor Cavarnos' remarkable educational history, from his primary education in Lesvos, Greece, his family homeland, to his secondary education at Boston English High School, in the city of his birth, as well as brief comments about his undergraduate and graduate education at Harvard. Additionally, he speaks of his professorial career at the University of North Carolina at Chapel Hill, at Wheaton College (in Norton, MA), at Hellenic College, at the Holy Cross Greek Orthodox School of Theology (where he taught in Greek), and at Clark University, and of his two years as a Fulbright Scholar in Greece, where he enjoyed wide acclaim for his research and was affiliated with the University of Athens.

A *scholar's scholar,* Cavarnos has produced a *scholar's reference* book that will please not only those in the specialized areas of academic research that it covers, but which will benefit anyone wishing to hone his use of specialized terminology in these same areas. All of us are immensely indebted to this fine scholar for a consummate new reference work that will be an indispensable aid to a generation of academics to come. I highly recommend it to students and scholars alike.

ARCHBISHOP CHRYSOSTOMOS
Center for Traditionalist
Orthodox Studies

III

PATRISTICS

1. *THE CONCEPT OF CHRISTIAN LOVE*

The Concept of Christian Love. Belmont, MA: Institute for Byzantine and Modern Greek Studies, 1995. Pp. 62 + Index.

It was with special joy that I received a copy of this book from the author, since, together with Father James Thornton, I published a short book on the subject of Christian love a few years ago, while teaching at the University of Uppsala, in Sweden: *Love*, the fourth volume in the series, *Themes in Orthodox Patristic Psychology* (Brookline, MA: Holy Cross Orthodox Press, 1989). This latter work, which approaches the subject of love from a psychological standpoint, using the writings of the Desert Fathers as a guide, is more speculative and broad in its approach than Professor Cavarnos' treatise. In fact, in kindly reviewing the original manuscript of our book, Dr. Cavarnos suggested some corrections in expression and several amplifications, without which Father James and I might have gone beyond the borders of intellectual speculation to a distortion of Orthodox Patristic teaching. If we owe him a debt of gratitude for these suggestions, we are especially obliged to him for producing a book which carefully and clearly defines Christian love from the standpoint of Scripture and the Patristic witness. Professor Cavarnos' book is an important and necessary counter-balance to our own book and other books like ours, which can be misunderstood without the firm footing in Orthodox teaching that Dr. Cavarnos' work provides.

In a handsomely-bound volume, taken from a lecture originally given by the author at Columbia University, Professor Cavarnos presents us with a general outline of Scriptural and Patristic teachings on the nature of love, the varieties of love, the relationship of love to the other spiritual virtues, and the special nexus between love and faith, the "foundation of all the other virtues of the soul" (p. 33). The book, which is available from the Institute for Byzantine and Modern Greek Studies (115 Gilbert Road, Belmont, Massachusetts 02478-2200), contains a Swedish text of the entire lecture (only the Preface to the book itself is missing from the Swedish text), which originally appeared in the Swedish theological journal *Nu Och Alltid* (No. 1, 1971). This is an especially happy circumstance for our Church, since we have a mission in Sweden that will without doubt greatly benefit from this excellent Swedish translation. We heartily recommend this excellent book, which is consistent with the high level of scholarship and spiritual insight that we have come to expect from works by Professor Cavarnos and from the publications of the Institute which he serves as President.

ARCHBISHOP CHRYSOSTOMOS
Center for Traditionalist
Orthodox Studies

2. *ST. PHOTIOS THE GREAT*

St. Photios the Great: Philosopher and Theologian. Belmont, MA: Institute for Byzantine and Modern Greek Studies, 1998. Pp. 84.

Patristics

This superb volume, a recent publication by one of the most learned Greek Orthodox writers of our times, treats of the seminal figure of St. Photios the Great, a Churchman who was both a great spiritual luminary of the Orthodox Church and, as the subtitle of the book indicates, a philosopher and theologian *extraordinaire*: a true Renaissance man, if I may characterize him in such an anachronistic manner.

The book consists of a monograph entitled "Saint Photios the Great as a Philosopher" and five "Reviews of Books on St. Photios": *viz.*, Father Asterios Gerostergios' *St. Photios the Great*; [Father] George Papademetriou's *Photian Studies*; the two separate volumes of St. Photios' Trinitarian works published by the Fraternité Orthodoxe Saint Grégoire Palamas; and Father Gerasimos Mikragiannanitis' *Akolouthía* in honor of the Saint.

Taken together, these materials offer an indispensable overview of an ecclesiastical personality whose life and works have maintained a vibrant relevancy for the whole of the Orthodox Church and for the intellectual world in general over many generations. We are all indebted to Professor Cavarnos for this contribution to the body of Orthodox scholarship in English. I am particularly indebted to the author for his gift of this work, kindly inscribed with his personal greetings.

ARCHBISHOP CHRYSOSTOMOS
Center for Traditionalist
Orthodox Studies

3. *THE PHILOKALIA*

The Philokalia. Belmont, MA: Institute for Byzantine and Modern Greek Studies, 2008. Pp. 340.

It was with the utmost joy that we received this magnificent volume of translations by Constantine Cavarnos of selected works from the first volume of *The Philokalia*. This is, indeed, a momentous publication and one of the finest among his numerous and invaluable contributions to the body of Orthodox theology available in English.

At the same time, precisely because these translations are of such sterling quality, our

delight is somewhat tempered by regret, in-
asmuch as Dr. Cavarnos did not translate the
entire work when he was younger. In almost
every book or article that he has written, he
cites *The Philokalia*. Indeed, not only has he
been reading and meditating on its contents
for many decades, but he has also endeavored
to apply its sublime precepts at a personal level.
An avid and lifelong practitioner of fasting, he
is distinguished by his chastity and temper-
ance, among his other virtues, and this moral
calibre, coupled with his outstanding knowledge of Greek in all of its diverse forms and his
general genius, makes him eminently qualified
to translate the whole of *The Philokalia*.

The contents of the volume under consideration are as follows: an Introduction by the
translator, the Proem (preface) by St. Nicodemos the Hagiorite, and selected writings by
St. Anthony the Great, St. Isaiah the Anchorite,
Evagrios the Monk, St. John Cassian, and St.
Mark the Ascetic (not including his "Epistle
to Nicholas the Solitary"). Thus, this book contains roughly two-thirds of the texts printed in
the first volume of the Greek original.

This brings me to a comparison between Dr. Cavarnos' translations and those contained in the ongoing English version of *The Philokalia*, under the able supervision of Metropolitan Kallistos (Ware) of Diokleia. It is not my intention to impugn the overall usefulness of this now standard translation of *The Philokalia*. We should, indeed, be very grateful to Metropolitan Kallistos and his coworkers (Dr. Cavarnos, it should be noted, was at one time an important translator among them) for making available for the first time in English a multitude of texts that were hitherto almost unknown outside traditionally Orthodox cultures.

However, a mere glance at the title page of each version suffices to show that Dr. Cavarnos is more faithful to the spirit of the original. His title page reads: *The Philokalia: Writings of Holy Mystic Fathers in which is Explained how the Mind is Purified, Illumined, and Perfected through Practical and Contemplative Ethical Philosophy.* By contrast, the other title page reads simply: *The Philokalia: The Complete Text.* So, from the very outset Dr. Cavarnos makes it abundantly clear that the aim of Sts. Makarios and Nicodemos in publishing *The Philokalia* was to guide the reader towards spiritual perfection, that is, deification ($\theta\acute{\epsilon}\omega\sigma\iota\varsigma$). This crucial point is not emphasized as clearly in the other version. Moreover, not a few reviewers of that version, including Archbishop Chrysostomos of Etna and the theologian Father Theodore Stylianopoulos, took its editors seriously to task for omitting the magisterial Proem by St. Nicodemos, in which he anchors *The Philokalia* in its authentic spiritual context. As Father Theodore points out, this Proem "breathes the air of patristic spiritual renewal" that undergirds the entire *oeuvre* of St. Nicodemos and his fellow *Kollyvades*.

Dr. Cavarnos is heartily to be commended for not relegating the work by St. Anthony to an appendix, as the editors of the *Complete Text* did, and for including St. Nicodemos' brief biographical notices of each author, which his erstwhile colleagues, for reasons best left to themselves, deemed inadequate or inappropriate. There are also no quasi-scholarly commentaries questioning the authenticity of this or that text in *The Philokalia*, which commentaries, aside from being tendentious and not always accurate, detract from the spiritual sobriety and purpose of the entire work.

The translations in this volume are, as one would expect, uniformly excellent. Their virtue, however, does not reside solely in their exceptional accuracy and fidelity to the original texts, or in their polished and dignified style, but also—and much more significantly—in their capacity to convey to the reader the Grace and beauty with which these incandescent spiritual writings are imbued. We will be forever indebted to Dr. Cavarnos for publishing this fine volume, incomplete though it may be, in which he splendidly succeeds in giving us much more than just a taste of the lavish spiritual fare of *The Philokalia*. This is Orthodox scholarship—any scholarship, for that matter—at its very best.

HIEROMONK PATAPIOS

Center for Traditionalist
Orthodox Studies

4. ST. MARK OF EPHESOS

St. Mark of Ephesos. With a Preface by Archbishop Chrysostomos of Etna. Belmont, MA: Institute for Byzantine and Modern Greek Studies, 2008. Pp. 81.

This excellent book on the "Atlas of Orthodoxy," St. Mark (Evgenikos) of Ephesos (*ca.* 1392-1444), first appeared in Greek in 1972. The Center for Traditionalist Orthodox Studies subsequently published a short monograph, in 1997, which I translated and compiled from the 1972 publication. The present English-language book is a revised and significantly enhanced form of the full original Greek text.

Archbishop Chrysostomos of Etna was asked to write the Preface for this new book, in which he emphasizes St. Mark's staunch fidelity to the Patristic and synodal traditions of Orthodoxy and to the spiritual principles of Hesychasm. He also acknowledges and analyzes, with absolute fair-mindedness and objectivity, the Saint's willingness to engage in honest debate with the Latins, which this great Confessor of the Faith did without compromising in any way his confession of the primacy of Orthodoxy. His Eminence's scholarly remarks complement Professor Cavarnos' trenchant analysis of St. Mark's importance in Orthodox history and indispensability for a proper understanding of the failed union dialogues with the Latin West.

I wish to note, with considerable satisfaction, that the Fathers of our monastery also assisted in the production of this splendid new edition by typesetting both the Greek and the English texts and by compiling the index. For all of us, this was a great honor and a small, yet sincere token of our profound appreciation to Dr. Cavarnos, not only for his many years of service on the Board of Advisors of the Center for Traditionalist Orthodox Studies and his steadfast friendship and support, but also for his outstanding contribution, as the unquestioned doyen of Greek Orthodox scholars in the English-speaking world, to the promotion of traditional Orthodox spirituality both as a cogent system of religious and ethical beliefs and actions and—no less importantly—

Patristics

as a viable way of life in the modern Western milieu.

Center for Traditionalist
Orthodox Studies

IV
PHILOSOPHY AND SCIENCE

1. *THE EDUCATIONAL PHILOSOPHY OF BENJAMIN OF LESVOS*

Ἡ περὶ παιδείας θεωρία τοῦ Βενιαμὶν Λεσβίου [*The Educational Philosophy of Benjamin of Lesvos*]. Athens: Ekdoseis "Orthodoxou Typou," 1984. Pp. 64.

Constantine Cavarnos has brought to the attention of Western scholars many significant and pivotal figures in Byzantine letters who have been injudiciously (and even systematically) ignored in general historical studies. One such figure is Benjamin of Lesvos, whose philosophy of education—I call his "theory" of education a "philosophy" of education—presents us with a clear portrayal of the subtle polish of the Byzantine-formed, modern Greek mind. That figures like Benjamin and studies like those of Cavarnos have not caused a revolution in Western thought is not so much a tragedy for Greek studies as it is for the modern West, which simply fails to benefit from an undiscovered source of intellectual wealth.

Benjamin of Lesvos flourished at the beginning of the nineteenth century and was instrumental in the introduction of the modern sciences into Greece. A man of wide learning, his philosophy of education extended over vast areas of human learning and was rooted in an understanding both of the ascendancy of man and the primacy of God. In many ways, his modern Greek educational theories reflect the Byzantine notion of man as the image of God—and thus worthy of study and attention in and of himself—and of God as an integral and transcendent element in the understanding of man. These anthropological and cosmological notions of "complementation," as it were, extend to learning, where Benjamin, educated in physics and mathematics, emphasizes the absolute importance and substance of philosophy (metaphysics) over the natural sciences— though, again, not in a tension-ridden scheme of opposing conceptualizations and theories, but in a complementary context of intellectual harmony.

In this small book, which I hope eventually to translate into English, with the author's permission, we find not only a *concise statement* of Benjamin's philosophy of education—set forth with the expertism, precision, and thoroughness typical of Cavarnos' scholarship—but a carefully *selected compendium* of passages from some of Benjamin's more important works.

I heartily recommend Dr. Cavarnos' little book to the scholar and general reader alike. It contains a wealth of information about a figure whose impact on our modern thinking is tragically limited. Books like this go a long way towards expanding our thought and overcoming such limitations.

BISHOP CHRYSOSTOMOS
Center for Traditionalist
Orthodox Studies

2. *THE HELLENIC-CHRISTIAN PHILOSOPHICAL TRADITION*

The Hellenic-Christian Philosophical Tradition. Belmont, MA: Institute for Byzantine and

Modern Greek Studies, 1989. Pp. 115 + Index.

The lectures in this book were originally delivered at Boston University under the sponsorship of the Department of Classical Studies and the Program in Modern Greek Studies. In what one can only call a brilliant synthesis of Greek thought, Dr. Cavarnos argues in these lectures that there is a continuum in Hellenic thought which binds classical Greek thought, the Greek Patristic tradition, and modern Greek philosophy together into a *single intellectual and spiritual whole.* A work of unparalleled scholarship—a work destined to be a classic among writings on intellectual history—this book carefully examines the role of Hellenic philosophy in serving the Greek Fathers and also the contributions of the Greek Fathers in transforming and correcting the limited truths of the Greek ancients. There emerges from this examination a clear understanding of the whole Greek experience, from Socrates, Plato, and Aristotle to the Greek Fathers of the Byzantine and present eras. This understanding reveals, in turn, the comprehensive Hellenic view of man, the universe, and God and its vital importance for the less developed course of Western philosophy. No philosopher, scholar, theologian, or simple Orthodox Christian should consider himself at all well read until he has studied this book in depth.

BISHOP CHRYSOSTOMOS
Center for Traditionalist
Orthodox Studies

3. *BIOLOGICAL EVOLUTIONISM*

Biological Evolutionism. Etna, CA: Center for Traditionalist Orthodox Studies, 1994. Pp. 34.

Professor Constantine Cavarnos is a renowned scholar, well known to Eastern Orthodox Christians in both the United States and Europe for his voluminous writings on such subjects as philosophy, religion, and history. He taught for many years at Harvard University, Wheaton College, Clark University, and other colleges and universities in this country, and has lectured before distinguished audiences around the world. Dr. Cavarnos, a philosopher, is uniquely equipped to write this monograph on evolutionism, since he deals with that theory as a philosophy: a faulty line of thought that masquerades as "proven scientific fact" and, moreover, one that forms the premise for a variety of ideologies that have brought immense tragedy to the world.

Dr. Cavarnos begins by discussing the two major schools of thought that dominate evolutionary thinking, the older being the school of Jean Baptiste Lamarck and the newer that of Charles Darwin. Lamarck published his *Philosophie Zoologique* fifty years before the appearance of Darwin's famed *Origin of the Species*. Both theories share much in common; however, the chief difference is that Lamarck taught that acquired characteristics could be inherited. In the Lamarckian scheme, giraffes have long necks and forelegs because aeons of stretching to reach edible foliage in trees supposedly elongated these bodily features permanently. This is, of course, sheer conjecture on Lamarck's part, and, as we now know, sheer balderdash as well. His observations not only cannot be proven, but, as the author points out, a critical flaw in the theory is neglected: overuse of bodily members or organs neither permanently changes the morphology of an organism nor allows temporary change to become heritable, and it can eventually cause debilitation. One who engages in great intellectual activity does not exhibit an increase in brain size, for example, nor is it true that one who repeatedly stretches to reach some object will experience increase in the length of the arms or legs. Such modifications as do come about, because of the exercise of muscle tissue, have no genetic ramifications and so are not passed on to future generations. Lamarckism is clearly not science but rank speculation of a most perilous kind. Writes the author:

> Viewed as a philosophical theory, Lamarck's evolutionism may be characterized as atheistic in substance, and as such subject to the criticisms to which atheism has been subjected through the ages by philosophers and theologians. Lamarck seeks to explain the origin of life and the existence of various species of

living things on our planet without reference to a cosmic plan or design, without reference to a World-Mind or God. He attempts to explain the appearance of life through *spontaneous generation*, and not as being a result of Divine creation. He neither offered nor could offer any real evidence or proof whatsoever of this view.

Lamarckian evolutionism assumes that environment is the crucial factor in evolution. That is why it remains popular, in renovated form, with liberals, communists, and other lovers of social engineering. Dr. Cavarnos comments:

> The reason why Neo-Lamarckism was favored in America and Soviet Russia over Darwinism was that Neo-Lamarckism served as a prop for the American and Soviet preconception that social 'progress' was to be achieved by changing the social environment through various manipulations. Thus, a *nonscientific* reason, a preconception, was involved in the espousing of Neo-Lamarckism.

Darwin accepted Lamarck's principle that life on Earth evolved from lower to higher forms and even countenanced aspects of the theory of the heritability of acquired character-istics. Yet, in contrast to the older scientist, Darwin explained the actual process of evolution differently, stressing "natural selection" and the "survival of the fittest" as primary mechanisms of change. Like Lamarck's hypothesis, however, Darwin's ideas are unproven, as Dr. Cavarnos illustrates, since no scientist has ever observed the sort of evolutionary change described in his books. Also like Lamarck, Darwin presupposes that various types of living creatures came into existence outside of any Divine plan.

Dr. Cavarnos asserts that evolutionary theory is not formulated according to the scientific method, which is supposed to be founded on an objective, impartial, and dispassionate examination of evidence. Rather, it is predicated on judgments that are almost entirely philosophical and metaphysical. Therefore, evolutionary theory is, at bottom, a type of naturalistic religion.

Transcendent or revelatory religions do not claim to be able to prove *empirically* all that they teach. It is not in the nature of religion to do this and people overly enamored of science are wont to criticize religion because it relies ultimately on faith. The same is true also of speculative philosophies that seek to explain the meaning of life or the universe. Faith, indeed, is one of the conspicuous distinctions between religion and philosophy, on the one hand, and science, on the other. People may be attracted to a religion or philosophy because it has a "ring of truth" about it, but to prove such truths in scientific fashion is usually not possible. What Dr. Cavarnos shows is that biological evolutionism is no different; though it uses the vocabulary of the physical sciences, its claims cannot be tested or demonstrated. Additionally, a preponderance of objective evidence seems to argue against many of its claims. Even the fossil record, viewed with objectivity, is not wholly supportive of the theory. And so, like religion, evolutionism requires a foundation of *faith* —the very thing that it attacks and derides.

Biological Evolutionism draws from the works of many philosophers, ancient and modern, to reveal the hollowness of both Lamarckism and

Darwinism. For readers wishing a concise yet devastating critique of evolutionism from an Orthodox Christian point of view, Dr. Cavarnos' excellent booklet is exactly what they have been seeking.

FATHER JAMES THORNTON
Center for Traditionalist
Orthodox Studies

4. *PYTHAGORAS ON THE FINE ARTS AS THERAPY*

Pythagoras on the Fine Arts as Therapy. Belmont, MA: Institute for Byzantine and Modern Greek Studies, 1994. Pp. 80.

Contemporary psychology has only recently discovered what is called the "Mozart effect," that is, an apparent relationship between certain sounds and rhythms—primarily those found in classical music—and an increase in spatial reasoning abilities. For the first time, thanks largely to the computer modelling of patterns and rhythms found in such classical compositions as those of Mozart and similar patterns and rhythms in the brain activity of subjects engaged in certain intellectual activities, there is empirical evidence that music affects our psychological state. Scientists have found that certain music—Western classical music, for example—enhances cognitive functioning and follows the rhythm and patterns of human brain activity, while music with rhythms and patterns discordant with those of brain activity—certain forms of "rock" music, for example—either does nothing to enhance, or interferes with, the reasoning process.

In a recently published book on the classical Greek philosopher Pythagoras († *ca.* 490 B.C.)—best known to Westerners for the hypotenuse theorem named after him (the square of the hypotenuse of a right triangle is always equal to the sum of the squares of its other two sides) and for so-called "Pythagorean" numbers, which follow a similar relationship (e.g., 5, 4, and 3: $5^2 = 4^2 + 3^2$)—Constantine Cavarnos makes some timely observations about the thinking of this Greek genius with regard to the fine arts—principally music—and their therapeutic value. In outlining the main features of his philosophy, Professor Cavarnos reveals to us the central function, among other principles, of *harmony* in all of Pythagoras' thinking. Indeed, Pythagoras believed, according to Cavarnos, that certain rhythms and melodies, endowed with harmonious beauty, were by nature therapeutic, affecting both the diseases of the body and imperfections in the reasoning powers of the soul.

It is interesting to note, if I may be allowed some oversimplification in recounting Dr. Cavarnos' very technical and precise exposition of Pythagoras' theories, that the latter had, in terms of modern psychophysiology, a very sophisticated understanding of the relationship between the body and the senses. In positing that certain musical sounds have a positive or therapeutic effect on the body, he clearly understood that music acts on the body through the mind; or, as we would say in modern terminology, he understood that the auditory stimuli associated with music affect the body through the mediation of cognitive processing, not simply through the senses. He also understood that not all sounds have the same therapeutic effect on the mind and body and that certain rhythms are more salutary than others. These observations are in complete accord with the "Mozart effect" in modern psychological research.

Superficial musicological scholars, most of them with a strong Western bias, have long argued for the existence of *direct* links between Byzantine music and Gregorian chant or certain Near Eastern musical traditions. In discussing Pythagoras' theory of the fine arts, Dr. Cavarnos makes reference to the direct relationship between the traditional chants of the Greek Orthodox Church and the modes of ancient Greek music, one of which, the Doric Mode, is thought to be the basis of the "First Tone" in Byzantine ecclesiastical music. The Church Fathers, like Pythagoras, also suggest that the traditional music of the Orthodox Church has therapeutic qualities, soothing the ills of both the body and the soul, as the author avers in an appendix of Patristic quotations. We are left with a convincing argument for the unique character of Byzantine chant, derived as it is directly from ancient Greek music, and with consequent collateral support for its claims to therapeutic qualities by way of the nexus between the observations of Pythagoras, a major theoretician of the classical fine arts, and modern psychological data. These insights make Cavarnos' book especially valuable to the Orthodox Christian and to those interested in the ecclesiastical traditions of the Orthodox Church.

I have touched only superficially on the superb exposition, in this remarkable book, of Pythagoras' treatment of the fine arts as therapy. I will leave it to the reader to study in detail Dr. Cavarnos' text, the short essay on ancient Greek music by the musicologist S. Karas, and the other excellent appendices attached to the book. This is one of the best treatments I have ever read of the philosophy of Pythagoras, his notions of the fine arts, and the relationship between Byzantine and ancient Greek theories of music. It is a rare and erudite work.

Bishop Chrysostomos
Center for Traditionalist
Orthodox Studies

5. *THE SEVEN SAGES OF ANCIENT GREECE*

The Seven Sages of Ancient Greece. Belmont, MA: Institute for Byzantine and Modern Greek Studies, 1996. Pp. 82.

The present book is the product of a series of lectures on the Pre-Socratic philosophers given by Professor Cavarnos at the University of North Carolina, Chapel Hill, and at the Institute for Byzantine and Modern Greek Studies. It is dedicated to seven of the pillars of ancient philosophy: Thales of Miletos, Pittacos of Mytilene, Bias (pronounced "Vias," in modern Greek) of Priene, Solon of Athens, Cleobulos of Lindos, Myson of Chen, and Chilon the Spartan. These "Seven Greek Sages"—with the exception of Thales, as Cavarnos notes—are seldom acknowledged by modern books on ancient Greek philosophy as *philosophers* (p. 11). Indeed, most literate Westerners are familiar only with Thales and Solon, the first as one of the fathers of astronomy, the second as the celebrated "Lawgiver of Athens." Nonetheless, all of these men were, above all else, philosophers; that is, they were sages and lovers and practitioners of wisdom. As Professor Cavarnos points out, the third-century historian of Greek philosophy Diogenes Laertios begins his book, *Lives and Opinions of Eminent Philosophers in Ten Books*, "with the Seven Sages and devotes many pages to them" (p. 12). Similarly, Plato, who was closer in time to these giants of classical wisdom, refers to them in one of his *Dialogues* ("Protagoras"), describing them (in words which he attributes to his master and teacher, Socrates) as "zealots" for wisdom.

Dr. Cavarnos discusses these philosophers in separate chapters devoted to each of them, and then adds a sampling of sayings from each in another chapter. The sayings are taken from the two-volume collection of philosophical, ethical, and spiritual writings, in Greek, published by St. Nectarios of Aegina in 1894 and 1895, his *Treasury of Sacred and Philosophical Sayings*. They are set out in a parallel text, with the original Greek placed side-by-side with a clear, precise translation into the English language by Dr. Cavarnos himself (pp. 64-79). The sayings evidence a profound concern among these ancient sages for the moral virtues and for wisdom that can, as the author notes in his Preface, "serve in every age and every country as a safe guide in one's individual and public life" (p. viii). This claim is borne out by a careful reading of the ancients' maxims, a few of which, for the sake of example, I will cite: "The universe is most beautiful, for it is a work of God" (Thales); "Exercise moderation" (Pittacos); "Blessed is he who is rich and enjoys the things he desires; but he who is free from desires is most blessed" (Bias); "Never desire to acquire a friend who can benefit neither the soul nor the body [i.e., prove beneficial to the preservation of the purity and integrity of the body]" (Solon); "The beginning of wisdom consists in the knowledge of one's ignorance" (Cleobulos); "...We should not investigate facts by the light of arguments, but arguments by the light of facts" (Myson); "When you suffer injustice, be reconciled, when you are insulted do not exact vengeance" (Chilon).

I have chosen to review this book in *Orthodox Tradition* for two reasons. First, in our times, few people are familiar with the classical

Greek roots of Western civilization. The majority of even educated people no longer read the Classics, so they are easily led to believe popular myths, such as those which associate the ancient Greeks with moral depravity or even perversion—things more quickly found in the effete scholars and writers who have misrepresented classical Greeks than in these forerunners of Christian wisdom themselves. It is especially important that, as Orthodox Christians, we understand the vision of moral virtue and personal uprightness taught by the ancient Greeks, since this vision was inspired by God and paved the way for the reception of Christianity by the ancient civilized world. If Christianity opened Paradise to mankind, the ancients were led by God to the "Door" through which we believers now freely pass. It is wrong for a believing Christian to accept the idea that pre-Christian Greek philosophy was practiced by men of moral depravity; it is also unjust, since this is not true, as the present book amply demonstrates.

My second reason for choosing this book for review is that it brings into focus the strong relationship between moral virtue as it was taught by the ancient Greek philosophers and as it is taught by the Orthodox Fathers. Even the most superficial observer cannot fail to see the similarity between the words of the Seven Sages and the sayings of the Desert Fathers, a similarity both in the content of their respective aphorisms and in their laconic, if not often ironic, style. It is no doubt simply because the purest wisdom of the ancients is at one with the wisdom of the Church Fathers—albeit, the former in shadow and the latter in vivid image—that St. Nectarios included the words of the Seven Sages in his collection of spiritual sayings. Indeed, St. Basil the Great, as Professor Cavarnos reminds us in his book (pp. 47-48), used a remark on virtue by Solon of Athens to set forth his own Christian directions on the desirability of acquiring virtue over the acquisition of possessions.

This noble book is enhanced by a useful Bibliography and a thorough, "reader-friendly" Index. Though lovers of the Classics will especially value it, it can be read with tremendous benefit to the mind and soul by any pious

Christian. It is a pleasure to read, filled, as it is, not with the little "cute" critical phrases and literary puns that characterize much popular scholarly writing, but with a sobriety and a singleness of purpose that are soul-building and edifying. This book offers *insight* into the sources of our civilization and Faith that every intelligent person should acquire.

ARCHBISHOP CHRYSOSTOMOS
Center for Traditionalist
Orthodox Studies

6. *PLUTARCH'S ADVICE ON KEEPING WELL*

Plutarch's Advice on Keeping Well. Belmont, MA: Institute for Byzantine and Modern Greek Studies, 2001. Pp. 70.

In this short but fascinating book, based on a lecture which he delivered at the International Congress of Psychopathology of Expression and Art Therapy, in September of 2000, at one of the teaching hospitals of his *alma mater,* Harvard University, Dr. Cavarnos sets forth the views of the famous Greek philosopher Plutarch (ca. 45-125 A.D.) on the subject of what today is known as wellness; that is, "the condition of good physical and mental health, especially when maintained by proper diet, exercise, and habits" (*American Heritage Dictionary of the English Language*, 3rd ed., 1996). This renowned classical Greek thinker devotes an entire treatise, *Advice on Keeping Well*, to the subject.

Plutarch's advice could be encapsulated in two of the more famous ancient Greek maxims, namely, "Γνῶθι σαυτόν" ("Know thyself") and "Μηδὲν ἄγαν" ("Nothing to excess"). Self-knowledge and the avoidance of extremes, as Plutarch points out in one of his letters, imply one another. Throughout his exposition, Dr. Cavarnos shows how Plutarch applied these precepts to many different aspects of daily life. For example, he recommends a diet consisting of "plain and familiar food," such as lentils, olives, vegetables, and fish, but cautions against excessive consumption of dairy products, and even suggests that meat be used only sparingly. Pious Orthodox Christians, who observe a similar kind of diet in fasting for a good part of the year, will be delighted to hear a pagan philosopher upholding the value of an ascetical practice which they know from experience to be tremendously beneficial, not only to the body, but also—and even more importantly—to the soul. Such good sense, coming as it does from one who was not a Christian, should put to shame those believers in our day who argue that fasting is detrimental to one's health.

Plutarch also makes many valuable comments about the need for moderation in sleep and rest and for taking proper care of one's body without unduly pampering it. It is noteworthy that he views the human person holistically, as a psychosomatic unity—an important insight which contemporary medical science has rediscovered.

In the second part of his book, Dr. Cavarnos presents extracts from other writings by Plutarch that shed additional light on the topics covered in the aforementioned treatise. Of particular interest is a passage from Plutarch's essay *On Tranquillity of Mind*, in which he points out that people spend much time examining works of art, but neglect to examine their own lives.

This edifying and inspiring book, like all of Dr. Cavarnos' publications, is attractively printed, and its value is further enhanced by two indices. I cannot recommend it too highly.

HIEROMONK PATAPIOS

Center for Traditionalist
Orthodox Studies

7. ARISTOTLE'S THEORY
OF THE FINE ARTS

Aristotle's Theory of the Fine Arts. Belmont, MA: Institute for Byzantine and Modern Greek Studies, 2001. Pp. ix + 94.

As has often been noted, Professor Cavarnos has a wonderful gift for presenting difficult philosophical and theological ideas in such a way that one who is not trained in either of these fields can appreciate their relevance to modern life. This new book on Aristotle reflects this gift and fittingly complements his earlier publications on the same theme, namely, *Pythagoras on the Fine Arts* (1994), *Plato's Theory of Fine Art* (2nd ed. 1998), and *Fine Arts as Therapy: Plato's Teaching Organized and Discussed* (1998).

More than one commentator has remarked, on the basis of his consistent emphasis on discerning and applying the mean in all areas of human life—and, thus, on avoiding excesses and deficiencies—that Aristotle must have been a very sane and balanced man. This impression is certainly confirmed by the author's brilliant interpretation of Aristotle's views on the fine arts. Dr. Cavarnos' long and profound immersion in the ancient Greek philosophical tradition is evident on every page of this fascinating study of a topic to which classical scholars and philosophers have devoted very little attention.

Aristotle considered the fine arts—such as literature, painting, sculpture, and music—to be essential components of any genuine educational program, the purpose of which was. for him, "the cultivation of all the virtues or excellences" (p. 41). One can only wonder what Aristotle would have thought of contemporary education, with its dreary utilitarian focus on preparing students to enter the job market, rather than on providing them with an "all-around education." A truly educated person, according to Aristotle, is acquainted with many different branches of knowledge and, "while not possessing the kind of proficiency which a specialist in each branch has, nevertheless is sufficiently at home in each branch to be able to exercise critical judgment in matters pertaining to it" (p. 53).

I have quoted at some length from Dr. Cavarnos' lucid summary of Aristotle's philosophy of education, since I believe that it shows clearly how very relevant classical Greek thought is to present-day concerns. Antique though it may seem, given its provenance in remote antiquity, it is anything but antiquated. It is one of the singular tragedies of the modern era that we have in many ways cut ourselves off, as a society, from our own cultural heritage, a heritage that is in large measure both shaped and defined by the sublime ideals and precepts of the classical Greek world.

Professor Cavarnos is to be commended for writing such an inspiring treatise on one of the greatest minds in history. It deserves to be widely read by all who cherish the classical tradition and its values, as well as by Orthodox Christians, who owe so much to the medium of classical Greek thought, through the language of which, by virtue of its "baptism" for that purpose, so much of the Church's more profound theology is expressed.

HIEROMONK PATAPIOS

Center for Traditionalist
Orthodox Studies

8. *ORTHODOXY AND PHILOSOPHY*

Orthodoxy and Philosophy. Belmont, MA: Institute for Byzantine and Modern Greek Studies, 2003. Pp. ix + 237.

Those who have read Dr. Cavarnos' superb account of the relationship between classical Greek philosophy and Patristic thought, *The Hellenic-Christian Philosophical Tradition*, will find his latest book, *Orthodoxy and Philosophy*, equally impressive. Based on lectures originally delivered by the author at St. Tikhon's Orthodox Theological Seminary in Pennsylvania, it covers some of the same ground as its predecessor, but explains in greater detail how individual Church Fathers made use of Platonic, Aristotelian, and Stoic philosophical categories and terminology in articulating their theological ideas. Thus, there are chapters dealing with the Apostolic Fathers, the Apologists, Clement of Alexandria, the Cappadocian Fathers, St. John Chrysostomos, St. Macarios of Egypt, St. Ephraim the Syrian, St. John Climacos, St. John of Damascus, St. Photios the Great, St. Symeon the New Theologian, St. Gregory Palamas, Patriarch Meletios (Pegas) of Alexandria, St. Nicodemos the Hagiorite, St. Nectarios of Aegina, and the twentieth-century Greek philosopher and religious thinker Nikolaos Louvaris. In the final chapter, the author surveys modern Western philosophy and evaluates it from an Orthodox perspective.

The chapter on St. Gregory Palamas is particularly important, since it provides a valuable corrective to the erroneous notion that St. Gregory was an obscurantist who dismissed secular learning as irrelevant to, or inconsistent with, Orthodox theology. The overall picture that emerges from Dr. Cavarnos' masterly analysis of the aforementioned Patristic writers is that they were generally more indebted to Plato than to Aristotle or the Stoics. To a greater or lesser extent, they all incorporated Aristotle's *Categories* into their theological thinking, but they seem otherwise to have found Plato's thought more congenial, especially in the areas of metaphysics and psychology. As Dr. Cavarnos points out, they do not call Aristotle "Divine," whereas they do, at times, apply this epithet to Plato; nor do they consider Aristotle superior to Plato, as Western Latin theologians typically did in the past. According to Louvaris, the centrality of the human soul in Platonic philosophy and the strong contrast that Plato makes between the sensible world and the spiritual world tend to render his thought more suitable than that of Aristotle as a vehicle for expressing the truths of the Orthodox Faith.

I would like to make a few observations regarding the chapter on Western philosophy. Dr. Cavarnos has, in the past, written widely and perspicaciously on such seminal modern philosophers as Henri Bergson and G.E. Moore. In view of this, it is a pity that he did not devote a separate book to the subject of Western philosophy. The chapter in question is filled with important and provocative insights, and this makes one wish that the author had set forth his views on modern philosophy at much greater length. Instead, Dr. Cavarnos singles out, for instance, what he sees as the pervasive vainglory that characterizes so much of European philosophy since the seventeenth century. He cites, for example, what George Santayana said about the thought of Kant, Hegel, Schopenhauer, and Nietzsche, among others; that is, that their philosophy is vitiated by a pervasive egotism. Santayana defines egotism, in this context, as "subjectivity in thought and willfulness in morals" (p. 182). While this may be true of Hegel, Schopenhauer, and Nietzsche, Kant, an intensely private and unassuming man who scarcely ever left his native Königsberg, would be difficult to place, at least unequivocally, in such company. A more expansive treatment of Western philosophy by Dr. Cavarnos would be very helpful, then, since it would no doubt provide the refinements and precision, with regard to these subtler issues in the Western philosophical tradition, for which he is so celebrated.

I have always found Dr. Cavarnos' writings to be immensely inspiring and instructive. Thus, I wholeheartedly recommend this new book to those interested in the nexus between philosophy and Orthodoxy. I also venture to hope, as I said, that Dr. Cavarnos will someday give us a more systematic assessment of modern Western philosophy from an Orthodox perspective. This would be of immense value and interest.

HIEROMONK PATAPIOS

Center for Traditionalist
Orthodox Studies

V

HELLENISM

1. *CULTURAL AND EDUCATIONAL CONTINUITY OF GREECE*

Cultural and Educational Continuity of Greece: From Antiquity to the Present. Belmont, MA: Institute for Byzantine and Modern Greek Studies, 1995. Pp. 58 + Appendix, Bibliography, and Index.

This book is based on a lecture delivered in May of 1993 by the distinguished Argentine philosopher, philologist, and Hellenist Saúl A. Tovar at the Institute for Byzantine and Modern Greek Studies in Belmont, MA. At the time, Dr. Tovar was conducting research at Harvard University, where Dr. Constantine Cavarnos, President of the Institute for Byzantine and Modern Greek Studies, studied and taught. The perhaps adventitious Harvard connections shared by Drs. Tovar and Cavarnos parallel the clear nexus between their studies of the Greek classics and Byzantine studies, something not at all accidental, since all good scholars share a single intention, that of shedding light on the truth by research and the collection, organization, and analysis of data.

Dr. Tovar's lecture, delivered in Greek, convincingly shows us that the classical Greek roots of Western civilization were never cut away from the tree of intellectual knowledge which grew up over them. They not only flourished after the classical era, but survived the fall of Byzantium into modern times. Characteristically, Dr. Tovar points out that the West, in its naïve and truncated view of intellectual history, forgets that, long before the foundation of the medieval universities of Western Europe, the University of Constantinople, established in 330 A.D., had revived and given continuity to the teaching traditions of Plato's Academy, Aristotle's Lyceum, and the *Mouseion* of Alexandria. The University of Constantinople also gave rise to other Greek educational institutions, including, in more modern times, the Patriarchal Academy, the Great School of the Nation, the Greek Academies of Romania, the Athonias School on Mt. Athos, and modern Greek educational institutions. The Greek intellectual and educational tradition, Tovar clearly establishes, has a continuous and unbroken history of development and is an integral part of the modern Western intellectual heritage.

Dr. Cavarnos' summary of Professor Tovar's lecture, edited and provided with an appendix on the Catechetical School of Alexandria, a useful bibliography, and an index, is a book which perfectly complements *The Hellenic-Christian Philosophical Tradition,* published by Professor Cavarnos in 1989 (Belmont, MA: Institute for Byzantine and Modern Greek Studies). I have without hyperbole stated in several publications that this latter book is one of the most important works ever written on the Western intellectual tradition. Like Dr. Tovar's lecture, it concerns itself with the neglected periods of Greek thought and philosophy, periods which, when properly studied and understood, provide us with vivid evidence for a tradition of thought that brings together antiquity and modernity—a unified Western cultural heritage that rises out of the continuity of the Greek and Christian intellectual experience.

Dr. Cavarnos' book on Professor Tovar's lecture, like his own book on the Hellenic-Christian intellectual experience, is of immense importance to the Orthodox Christian. The continuous witness of the Greek intellectual world is an important part of our Western scholarly tradition. But transformed as it was by Orthodox Christianity, it is also an important part of our spiritual and religious tradition. If Westerners are woefully ignorant of the origins of their intellectual traditions, they are similarly appallingly ignorant of the Orthodox roots of their religious traditions. Books like these put Orthodox primacy in perspective, helping us to understand that it is based not on provincial claims to religious superiority or political attempts at worldly dominance, but on firm historical and philosophical foundations. I heartily recommend this informative, handsome, and very readable book.

BISHOP CHRYSOSTOMOS
Center for Traditionalist
Orthodox Studies

2. *THE HELLENIC HERITAGE*

The Hellenic Heritage: Two Lectures Dealing with Greek Culture: Ancient, Byzantine, and Modern. Belmont, MA: Institute for Byzantine and Modern Greek Studies, 1999. Pp. 128.

In this, his most recent publication, Dr. Cavarnos demonstrates yet again his consummate expertise in presenting Greek culture in all of its phases. In many of his other writings, most notably *Byzantine Thought and Art, The Hellenic-Christian Philosophical Tradition,* and *Cultural and Educational Continuity of Greece,* he has covered much of the material discussed in this new book. In this work, however, he provides the reader with a magnificent synthesis of this material, drawn from the rich learning that he has amassed over a period of more than six decades of scholarly research. Indeed, for a number of reasons, I believe that it is one of the better of the many outstanding books that he has written.

To begin with, the author shows conclusively, as the title of one of the aforementioned books indicates, that authentic Greek culture, with its uninterrupted legacy of nearly three thousand years, is not only the most sublime expression of the human spirit that has ever existed, but also—and more importantly, from an Orthodox point of view—constitutes the intellectual and spiritual soil in which Christianity put down its roots and thereby overcame the world. I say authentic Greek culture, because much of what passes for Greek culture in our day and age, especially in America, with its exaltation of Zorba, *ouzo*, and *baklava(s)*, has, in reality, little or nothing to do with the profound and sober culture exemplified by such luminaries as Plato and Aristotle, the Cappadocian Fathers, St. Gregory Palamas, St. Nicodemos the Hagiorite, and Evgenios Voulgaris, to name but a few out of the many outstanding figures who adorn the pages of this book.

In the second place, although the term παιδεία (*paideia*), as Dr. Cavarnos astutely observes, means far more than simply "education," his painstaking research into Greek history and civilization proves, beyond any doubt, that, in whatever country they have found themselves living, true Greeks have always made it a top priority to establish schools or academies to promote not only the Greek language, in both its ancient and more modern forms, and Greek philosophy and theology, but also a wide range of secular disciplines and foreign languages. For example, at the renowned Evangeliki School in Smyrna, St. Nicodemos learned French, Latin, and Italian, and was thus afforded the means of becoming "acquainted with Western European religious and philosophical thought" (p. 79). It is also worthy of note that many Greek theological texts, such as those of Damaskenos the Studite and Agapios Landos, were translated into Russian, Bulgarian, or Romanian. This fact alone offers us a glimpse into Orthodoxy's healthier, cosmopolitan past, into an era of genuine pan-Orthodox unity in which the anti-Christian heresy of phyletism or ethnicism was completely unknown.

Thus, Dr. Cavarnos did well to entitle this book *The Hellenic Heritage* rather than *The Greek Heritage*. The phenomenon of Hellenism wholly transcends the present-day national boundaries of Greece and the sometimes provincial preoccupations which, unfortunately, cloud the wider dimensions of the Greek witness in the letters, science, and theology. In theological terms, as the late Father Georges Florovsky never tired of repeating, the notion of Hellenism entails all that is Orthodox, regardless of national origin: all that which belongs to a single family, the spiritual ancestors of which are the Greek Fathers. It is just such a universal Hellenism that one finds in the pages of this superb new work by Dr. Cavarnos.

Thirdly, the author decisively lays to rest the misapprehension, all too common among Western classicists, that Hellenic culture petered out somewhere around the late third century. It also undermines the bizarre notion that Greek is a "dead" language, a piece of scholarly chicanery which is supposedly validated by the "Erasmian" pronunciation that still prevails in university Classics departments outside Greece. I was also most interested to learn of the important contributions to the study of ancient Greek philosophy made by two prominent modern Greek philosophers, Ioannis Theodorakopoulos and Konstantinos Georgoulis. Their works should be translated into English, in order to show that there are Greek intellectuals who take their heritage seriously and who, in particular, respect the philosophical achievements of their ancestors. This would certainly provide a valuable counterweight to the prevailing analytic approach to the ancient Greek thinkers, characteristic of Anglo-American philosophy, which tends to foster a very condescending attitude towards the Pre-Socratics, Plato, and Aristotle.

Like all of Dr. Cavarnos' publications, *The Hellenic Heritage* is attractively produced, clearly written, and contains helpful indices. Throughout his distinguished career, as I tell my own students, the author has displayed a remarkable ability to make complex ideas accessible to non-specialists and to interpret the rich treasures of Christian Hellenism for the English-speaking world. This superb book is no exception to his fine work, and it deserves to be widely read.

ARCHBISHOP CHRYSOSTOMOS
Center for Traditionalist
Orthodox Studies

3. GREEK LETTERS AND ORTHODOXY

Greek Letters and Orthodoxy: Their Relations During Two Millennia. Belmont, MA: Institute for Byzantine and Modern Greek Studies, 2004. Pp. vii + 60.

This fine book is a tribute to the historical and cultural percipience of a scholar who has, for many decades now, employed his learned mastery of matters philosophical, theological, and linguistic to the explication and understanding of the Orthodox Faith and its Saints and principal clerical and secular expositors and apologists—and this in a catholic, inclusive way, writing on Orthodox figures from every national tradition. In the volume at hand, a much appreciated gift which the author personally inscribed, Professor Cavarnos concentrates on the particular traditions of the Greek Church and the "significant relations," to quote the subtitle on the title page of the volume, "of Orthodox Christianity to the Greek language and to ancient Greek philosophy, rhetoric, and poetry." As such, the work is not in the genre of those naive essays putting forth the anserine idea—a by-product of the ethnic myopia of phyletism—that this-or-that language is "Divine" and somehow endowed with the inherent ability to convey theological and spiritual truths which, in keeping with the apophatic traditions of the Christian East, are actually contained in knowledge that is not knowledge and which, quite obviously, transcend human language. Rather, in a respected intellectual tradition, Dr. Cavarnos intelligently, persuasively, and clear-sightedly argues that the richness of the Greek language, ancient Greek literature and philosophy, and the rhetorical traditions of the classical Hellenic world served to *capture* and *express* the knowable aspects of Christianity, from Scripture itself to the credal and Synodal pronouncements of the Church and the writings of the Greek Fathers.

In two chapters on classical Greek philosophical models and rhetoric, the author demonstrates that the Christian Church, in setting out its revealed truths through the vehicle of Greek letters, was selective and careful in how it adopted, adapted, and "baptized," as it were, the cultural elements of classical Hellenism to the service of Christian apologetics and theology. He notes, for example—citing St. Basil the Great—that one must be discriminating and eclectic in taking from the Classical poets that which is conducive to good comportment of a Christian kind and avoiding that which constitutes "base conduct." Nonetheless, he points out that the very intellectual structure of Orthodox Christianity was formed and molded around these elements of Classical thought and literature. Dr. Cavarnos goes on, in his third and final chapter, to affirm that Greek letters are "relevant" to our day, since the Greek language is helpful in understanding, and in the hermeneutical expatiation of, Scripture (for which reason it is almost always studied in theological seminaries in every Christian country). Greek philosophy also assists theology, in helping to form ideas and thoughts with analytical precision—the hallmark of such Greek philosophy. As for Greek rhetoric and poetry, the richness of the Church's liturgical and hymnographic traditions, alone, attests to this and to what the author calls the "perennial value" of these ancient literary devices.

Hellenism

This is a wonderful book worthy of a thorough reading.

ARCHBISHOP CHRYSOSTOMOS
Visiting Scholar,
Program in Comparative Religion
University of Washington, Seattle

77

VI

PHOTIOS KONTOGLOU

1. *MEETINGS WITH KONTOGLOU*

Συναντήσεις μὲ τὸν Κόντογλου [*Meetings with Kontoglou*]. Athens: Astir, 1985. Pp. 221.

If Constantine Cavarnos has earned a reputation in both the United States and Greece for his outstanding contributions to Byzantine studies and Orthodox scholarship in general, his reputation is one that closely associates him with the renowned Greek scholar and iconographer Photios Kontoglou. It should surprise no one, then, to see this present book of personal reflections on Dr. Cavarnos' many meetings with his friend and spiritual colleague. It constitutes an expression of his deep appreciation for Kontoglou's Orthodox witness, a witness lauded in many of Cavarnos' books and formally marked by a series of essays (in Greek) written two years after Kontoglou's death in 1965, *Hellas kai Orthodoxia* (Athens, 1967), by Cavarnos.

In his accounts of various personal encounters with Kontoglou, Dr. Cavarnos gives us a glimpse into the mature years of this great man, from about 1950 to his repose. There is a wide presentation of Kontoglou's thoughts and impressions on various subjects, leaving the reader with a clear impression of the man as iconographer, as author, as philosopher, and, most importantly, as a paradigmatic Orthodox Christian. Cavarnos' observations are set forth in an easy style, lucidly, and wholly ingenuously. The man who was Kontoglou therefore emerges from these accounts as a real human being, not as the would-be hero of an admiring scholar's overstatement. I have seldom read such an enjoyable book about any contemporary figure, free as it is from the tendency to treat recent figures with the exaggerated intimacy or contrived objectivity prompted by temporal proximity.

Of the many meetings reported by Dr. Cavarnos, several struck me especially. I was fascinated by the trips he made with Kontoglou to the monastery directed by the blessed Archimandrite Philotheos (Zervakos) on the island of Paros (*Hiera Mone Longovardas*), since Father Philotheos, the spiritual son of Saint Nectarios of Aegina, was the spiritual father of my own spiritual father, Metropolitan Cyprian of Oropos and Fili. Photios Kontoglou's respect for, and assessment of, the spiritual wisdom of Father Philotheos, as reported in Cavarnos' reminiscences, call to mind all that I have heard of this great Elder, as well as my one encounter with Father Philotheos at a lecture many decades ago in Thessaloniki. Just as Cavarnos' visit to this famous monastery on Paros was "enough to confirm the opinion held about it and its abbot by Kontoglou" (p. 34), so his words were adequate to spark in my own memory fond and sympathetic feelings towards the same. Such is the sign of a good book—especially one with spiritual impact.

In another chapter, Dr. Cavarnos tells of his meeting, at the invitation of Kontoglou and his wife on a certain feast day, with various young students from the Orthodox Church of Uganda, about which Kontoglou wrote several articles. We gain here some insight into the missionary zeal of Photios Kontoglou and his grasp of

the catholicity of Orthodoxy—something often
ignored by Western converts and superficial
Orthodox, who find, in his uncompromising
comments about the ascendency of Orthodox
spirituality (see, for example, the translation
of his comments on Eastern Orthodoxy and
Roman Catholicism in my book, *Orthodoxy and
Papism*), what they quite mistakenly characterize as a cultural (Greek) bias. We must remem-
ber that the same Kontoglou who understood
and extolled Orthodox Christianity as the very
criterion of Christian wisdom could also write
with appreciation about no less a Westerner
than Blaise Pascal (see his book *Pege Zoes*) and
embrace his African brothers.

Because I have an enduring interest in the
great Russian writer Fyodor Dostoyevsky, I
was interested in the chapter in this book dedicated to Kontoglou and Cavarnos' joint fas-
cination with this figure. I will leave it to the
reader to judge this exciting chapter for himself,
offering only this tantalizing summary of Dostoyevsky's work, related to Professor Cavarnos, in one of his discussions on the subject, by
Kontoglou: "Dostoyevsky has a depth which

Westerners do not possess. Western authors are generally superficial, remaining only on the surface [of things]" (p. 167).

The photographs in this book are a treasure in themselves. Every reader will be delighted in them. The book is handsome, durably bound in paper, and carefully printed. My copy, a much appreciated gift from the author himself, is something which I shall cherish. I heartily recommend this book to every Orthodox Christian with a reasonable knowledge of Greek. I look forward to an English edition of the book, which should give English-speaking Orthodox (and others) in the West a charming glance into the Orthodox world of no less a traditionalist than the man who almost single-handedly restored Byzantine iconography to our churches in this century: the blessed and ever-memorable Photios Kontoglou. The great and growing debt that we owe to Professor Cavarnos is substantially increased by his writing of this remarkable book.

BISHOP CHRYSOSTOMOS OF OREOI
Center for Traditionalist
Orthodox Studies

Photios Kontoglou

Meetings with Kontoglou. Belmont, MA: Institute for Byzantine and Modern Greek Studies, 1992. Pp. xi + 214.

The Greek-language text of this inspiring portrait of the ever-memorable Photios Kontoglou, which was published in Athens in 1985, has already been given an excellent review by Bishop Chrysostomos of Etna (*The Greek Orthodox Theological Review,* 32 [1987]: 436-438). However, for the benefit of those readers who did not see His Eminence's appraisal, I shall offer a few observations of my own about the English-language text of the book.

The contents of this book are aptly summarized by its subtitle: "Enlightening, lively discussions on Byzantine iconography and music, diverse writers, philosophers and theologians, and contemporary events and trends, between the author and the great icon painter, writer, and philosopher Photios Kontoglou." Kontoglou is probably best known in the West as someone who almost single-handedly restored traditional Byzantine iconography to its rightful preëminence, not only championing its authenticity in contrast to the second-rate imitations of Italian Renaissance painting that were so popular in Greece and much of the Orthodox world earlier in this century, but also putting his theories into practice. Numerous examples of Kontoglou's icons, frescoes, and sketches are to be found in this work, as in other books on Byzantine iconography by Dr. Cavarnos. What emerges clearly from these memoirs is a much more rounded portrait of this very pious and cultivated Orthodox layman, who was a distinguished man of letters—the first volume of his *Works (Aivali, My Native Place)* was awarded the prestigious Purfina Prize—an *aficionado* of Byzantine music, and a theologian in his own right.

Kontoglou was devoted above all to Holy Tradition in all of its forms. He was not afraid of chiding even Patriarch Athenagoras of Constantinople for having given an organ to a church in Corfu and for attempting to install one in Crete (pp. 84-85). It is evident that he had very little respect for what passed in his day as academic, supposedly "scientific" theology. He exposed the "pseudomorphosis" of modern Greek theology, just as Father Georges Florovsky did for Russian theology. He knew full well that the truths of Orthodoxy must be experienced and lived, and he put this awareness into practice as much in theology as he did in traditional iconography. His way of life was modest—he did not have so much as a savings account, let alone a pension—and was founded entirely upon the precepts of the Church. We may find it hard to believe, given the breadth of culture manifested in Dr. Cavarnos' conversations with this contemporary pillar of Orthodoxy, but Kontoglou maintained that he was "a primitive man, …not versed in philosophies and such things" (p. 56). Such humility is perhaps encountered most of all in those who are truly great and therefore have no need to give themselves "airs." What Kontoglou said of Papa Nicholas Planas, who was glorified last year by the Œcumenical Patriarchate, can also be applied to Kontoglou himself: "Many should read this book on [in this instance, Photios Kontoglou], because they will be moved seeing how simple and sweet authentic Greek Orthodoxy is" (p. 184).

This is altogether a wonderful book. The quality of the layout and printing is fully up to the standards that we have come to expect from the Institute for Byzantine and Modern Greek Studies. What makes it especially impressive is that it comes from the pen of one who knew Kontoglou personally and spent many hours conversing with him. My only regret is that Dr. Cavarnos did not include his moving obituary to Kontoglou, which was printed in *The Orthodox Word* (1966). This eloquent tribute supplies the biographical details missing from *Meetings with Kontoglou*. We can only hope that in the coming years, Dr. Cavarnos will make more of Kontoglou's writings available in English.

PATRICK G. BARKER

Lecturer in Sacred Languages
St. Joseph of Arimathea
Anglican Theological College

2. ANTI-PAPIST WRITINGS

Φωτίου Κόντογλου, Ἀντιπαπικά. Ἀθῆναι: Ἐκδόσεις «Ὀρθοδόξου Τύπου», 1993. Σελίδες: 96.

Photios Kontoglou

Ὁ καθηγητὴς πανεπιστημίου κ. Κωνσταντίνος Καβαρνός, ἀπὸ δεκαετίας συνεργάτης μας εἰς τὸ Κέντρον Παραδοσιακῶν Ὀρθοδόξων Σπουδῶν, εἶναι γνωστὸς τόσον εἰς τὴν Ἀμερικὴν ὅσον καὶ εἰς τὴν Ἑλλάδα, ἀπὸ πολλὰ βιβλία καὶ ἄρθρα του, τὸ παραδοσιακὸν Ὀρθόδοξον φρόνημά του καὶ τὴν ἀξιοσημείωτον λογιότητά του. Τὸ πρόσφατον ἔργον τοῦ Καθηγητοῦ Καβαρνοῦ, μία συλλογὴ ὅλων τῶν ἀντιπαπικῶν ἀνοικτῶν ἐπιστολῶν καὶ ἄρθρων τοῦ μακαριστοῦ Φ. Κόντογλου, τὰ ὁποῖα ἔχουν δημοσιευθῆ εἰς τὴν γνωστὴν ἑλληνικὴν ἐφημερίδα «Ὀρθόδοξος Τύπος» μεταξὺ 1963 καὶ 1970, δεικνύει ὅτι ἀνθίζει ἀκόμη ἡ ἐκδοτικὴ δραστηριότης τοῦ κ. Καβαρνοῦ: ἐκ τοῦ τελευταίου τούτου βιβλίου τοῦ Δρ Καβαρνοῦ ἀντλοῦμεν τὸ θέμα τῆς παρούσης συντόμου κριτικῆς.

Τὰ συγκεντρωμένα γράμματα καὶ δοκίμια τοῦ Κόντογλου εἰς τὸ βιβλιαρίδιον τοῦτο, μὲ πρόλογον καὶ σημειώσεις τοῦ κ. Καβαρνοῦ, ἀποτελοῦν μίαν καθαρὰν ἔκφρασιν τοῦ πνεύματος τῶν ἁγίων Πατέρων μας σχετικῶς μὲ τὴν προφανῆ ἀπάτην, τὴν ὑποστηρίζουσαν

τὴν βλάσφημον θεωρίαν τοῦ παπικοῦ πρω-
τείου, ὡς καὶ τὰς ἄλλας "ἀνοησίας"—καθὼς
γράφει ὁ Κόντογλου (σ. 42)—τοῦ παπισμοῦ.
Εἰς τὴν συλλογὴν αὐτὴν τῶν προφητικῶν
ἀντιπαπικῶν κειμένων τοῦ μακαριστοῦ
Φωτίου, δύναται νὰ ἴδη ὁ Ὀρθόδοξος Χρι-
στιανὸς τῆς διακρίσεως, ὅτι ὁ παπισμὸς θέτει
εἰς φρικτὸν κίνδυνον—καὶ ἰδιαιτέρως εἰς τὸν
σημερινὸν κόσμον—τὴν Πίστιν μας καὶ τὴν
πνευματικὴν καὶ ἐθνικήν μας παράδοσιν. Τὰ
κείμενα τοῦ Κόντογλου μᾶς ὑπενθυμίζουν
τὴν καταδίκην τοῦ παπισμοῦ ἀπὸ τὴν
Ὀρθόδοξον Ἐκκλησίαν, καὶ τά γράμματά του
πρὸς τοὺς τότε ἡγέτας τῆς ἐκκλησίας, διὰ τῶν
ὁποίων τοὺς κατακρίνει διὰ τὰ φιλοπαπικὰ
των αἰσθήματα, ἔχουν μεγάλην σημασίαν
διὰ τὴν σημερινὴν Ὀρθόδοξον Ἐκκλησίαν.
Καὶ τοῦτο, διότι σήμερον ἔχει φθάσει εἰς τὸ
σημεῖον νὰ θεωρῆ τὸν ἑαυτόν του ἕτερον
"πάπαν" τῆς Ἀνατολῆς ὁ Πατριάρχης τῆς
Μεγάλης Ἐκκλησίας, ὁ δῆθεν primus inter
pares (πρῶτος ἐν ἴσοις). Ἂς ἐλπίσωμεν, ὅτι
δὲν θὰ ἀποτολμήση τὸ ἑπόμενον βῆμα, μι-
μούμενος τὸν ὁμόλογόν του τῆς Ρώμης, νὰ

Photios Kontoglou

ἀνακηρύξῃ ἑαυτὸν "servum servorum Dei" (δοῦλον τῶν δούλων τοῦ Θεοῦ)! Ὁ κίνδυνος πλέον δὲν εἶναι ἁπλῶς ἐντὸς τῆς αὐλῆς τῆς Ἐκκλησίας, ἀλλὰ ἔχει κυριεύσει δυστυχῶς, λόγῳ τῆς οἰκουμενικῆς κινήσεως, τὸν πρῶτον θρόνον τῆς Ὀρθοδοξίας.

Ὡς ἐκ τούτου, αἰσθανώμεθα ἰδιαιτέρως ὑποχρεωμένοι εἰς τὸν κ. Καβαρνὸν διὰ τὸ λίαν σημαντικὸν τοῦτο βιβλίον, τὸ ὁποῖον πρέπει νὰ γίνῃ τὸ "Κόκκινον Βιβλίον" τῶν γνησίων Ὀρθοδόξων Χριστιανῶν εἰς τὴν δύσκολην ἔνστασιν τῶν ἡμερῶν μας ἐναντίον τῶν δαιμονικῶν πολιτικῶν δυνάμεων τοῦ παπισμοῦ.

Ἐπίσκοπος Ἔτνα Χρυσόστομος
Κέντρον Παραδοσιακῶν
Ὀρθοδόξων Σπουδῶν

Φωτίου Κόντογλου, Ἀντιπαπικά [The Anti-Papist Writings of Photios Kontoglou]. Athens, Greece: "Orthodoxos Typos" Editions, 1993. Pp. 96.*

89

NEW LIBRARY

Professor Constantine Cavarnos, an associate of ours at the Center for Traditionalist Orthodox Studies for some ten years, is known both in America and in Greece for his many books and articles, his traditional Orthodox outlook, and his remarkable erudition. The present work by Professor Cavarnos, a collection of all of the anti-papist open letters and articles of the blessed Photios Kontoglou that appeared in the well-known Greek periodical Ὀρθόδοξος Τύπος between 1963 and 1970, testifies to the prodigious scope of his publication efforts. It is from this latest book by Dr. Cavarnos that we take the subject of the present brief review.

The collected letters and essays of Kontoglou in this small book, with a prologue and notes by Dr. Cavarnos, constitute a clear expression of the spirit of the Holy Fathers with regard to the obvious deceit which underlies the blasphemous theory of papal primacy, as well as the other "stupidities"—as Kontoglou writes (p. 42)—of papism. In this collection of prophetic, anti-papist texts, the perceptive Orthodox Christian can see that papism places our Faith and our ethnic traditions—especially in the contemporary world—in jeopardy. Kontoglou's articles remind us that papism has been condemned by the Orthodox Church. Kontoglou's letters to the then-leaders of the Church, in which he chastises them for their pro-papist sentiments, also have great significance for the contemporary Church, for today we have reached the point that the Patriarch of Constantinople, the so-called *primus inter pares* ("first among equals"), has come to consider himself another Pope, the Pope of the East. Let us hope that he will not risk a further step, in imitation of his counterpart in Rome, and declare himself *servum servorum Dei* ("servant of the servants of God" [that is, Christ Himself])! Danger, indeed, no longer awaits us just in the courtyard of the Church, but has unfortunately overcome the first Throne of the Orthodox Church.

We feel particularly indebted to Dr. Cavarnos, then, for this very significant book, one which should become the "Red Book" of True Orthodox Christians in the difficult resistance

of our times against the demonic political forc-
es of papism.

Bishop Chrysostomos
Center for Traditionalist
Orthodox Studies

* This review originally appeared in Greek (*vide
supra*) in *The Hellenic Voice* (February 1994). It was
subsequently published in English in *Orthodox
Tradition*.

3. *SOUL-PROFITING TEACHINGS*
OF PHOTIOS KONTOGLOU

Ψυχωφελεῖς Διδαχαὶ τοῦ Φωτίου Κόντογλου
[*Soul-Profiting Teachings of Photios Kontoglou*].
Athens: "Orthodoxos Typos" Publications,
2002. Pp. 63.

Photios Kontoglou is justifiably renowned,
both in Greece and elsewhere, for his almost
single-handed efforts to restore the authentic
Byzantine iconographic tradition to the Orthodox Church. However, he was just as much a
man of letters and an astute theological writer, as is evident from the six volumes of his

collected works published some years ago in Athens. Unfortunately, very little of this valuable material has been translated into English, and efforts to continue publishing Kontoglou's work have been sporadic.

We can thus be very grateful to Dr. Constantine Cavarnos for his diligence, in the present volume, in compiling some of the numerous articles that Kontoglou contributed to the religious newspaper Ὀρθόδοξος Τύπος and in making more of this brilliant thinker's works available. This is the fourth volume in Cavarnos' series of anthologies of Kontoglou's writings, consisting of six essays on a variety of topics. The initial essay, "The Hidden Treasure and the Pearl of Great Price," is a beautiful meditation on the Kingdom of God, for which Kontoglou draws heavily upon the writings of St. Isaac the Syrian, St. Dionysios the Areopagite, and St. Symeon the New Theologian. The second essay is a review by Kontoglou of a book on the crisis through which Athonite monasticism passed in the early 1960s. Kontoglou makes some very telling criticisms of certain ideas put forth by the author of that book, Father Gregory (Atsalis). To capture the spirit of this review, we might cite Kontoglou's comments on Father Gregory's thesis that this crisis was caused by a lack of love on the part of monastic superiors towards the monks under obedience to them. Kontoglou observes, in response to Father Gregory, that the latter would also do well to show more love towards their superiors.

The third essay in the book is a very literate modern Greek translation of the *Discourse on the Monastic Life* by Metropolitan Theoleptos of Philadelphia, a mentor of St. Gregory Palamas. Following a brief but lucid explanation, in the fourth essay, of the Icon of St. John the Forerunner, the fifth essay is an encomium by Kontoglou to St. Tarasios of Constantinople, the great Confessor of the Holy Icons. The sixth and final essay concerns the renowned short story writer Alexandros Papadiamantis, the "Saint of Greek letters," whose virtues of simplicity, humility, kindness, and faith Kontoglou exhorts his countrymen to emulate.

I venture to hope that Dr. Cavarnos will someday publish English translations of these and other essays by Kontoglou. In the meantime, I look forward eagerly to the fifth and final volume in this excellent series.

HIEROMONK PATAPIOS
Center for Traditionalist
Orthodox Studies

4. *FINE ARTS AND TRADITION*

Fine Arts and Tradition: A Presentation of Kontoglou's Teaching. Belmont, MA: Institute for Byzantine and Modern Greek Studies, 2004. Pp. xv + 96.

Dr. Cavarnos has performed a considerable service to the English-speaking Orthodox world by making available a fascinating and inspiring collection of Photios Kontoglou's writings on the fine arts. This book contains four essays by Kontoglou entitled, respectively, "Free Art and Tradition," "The Orthodox Tradition of Iconography," "Classical Greek Art," and "Ancient Art and Byzantine Art." Dr. Cavarnos, who knew Kontoglou personally and frequently conversed with him on a wide variety of subjects, provides the reader with a very lucid and helpful introduction to the thinker's general theory of art. There are also two interesting appendices: "A Self-Portrait of Photios Kontoglou" (a summary by Kontoglou of his literary and artistic *oeuvre*) and "The Workshop of Photios Kontoglou" (a brief account of Kontoglou's pupils and disciples).

It is important to emphasize that Kontoglou, for all of his ostensible coolness towards things Western, was no bigot. Not only did he condemn chauvinism, which he regarded as the "fanatical and stupid restriction of an artist to a small circle of ideas and values" (p. 20), but he also had a genuine appreciation for classical cultures like those of Egypt, India, China, and Japan, all of which were steeped in tradition. This is the context in which we should understand Kontoglou's rather critical estimation of Western painting—specifically that of the Italian Renaissance. We need not suppose that Kontoglou, with his deep knowledge of Western art, would have dismissed *all* of the painting produced by the Italian masters in

this period. What bothered him about the Renaissance was its break with tradition and its
tendency to promote an excessively subjectiv-
ist and arbitrary approach to art.

I heartily recommend this splendid new
book by Professor Cavarnos to anyone who is
deeply interested in art history or in the relationship between aesthetics and theology and
the art of the Renaissance.

HIEROMONK PATAPIOS

Center for Traditionalist
Orthodox Studies

VII

SPIRITUAL LIFE

1. *FASTING AND SCIENCE*

Fasting and Science. Trans. Bishop Chrysostomos and Hieromonk Auxentios. Etna, CA:
Center for Traditionalist Orthodox Studies.
1988. Pp. 21.

The subject of fasting is an important one
for Orthodox Christians. Fasting lies at the
core of the spiritual practices of our Church.
Contemporary notions about fasting—that it
is in the domain of the monastic, that it is subject to personal choice and voluntary, and that
it is unhealthy—have helped to undermine
its practice among contemporary Orthodox
Christians, and the devastating effect of this
decline in practical piety has taken its toll on
the Church. It is thus all the more crucial in
our times that this important subject be understood and studied by all of the members of the
Orthodox Church, whether monastics, clergy,
or lay people.

Dr. Cavarnos has supplied us with a precise, exhaustive, and brilliant commentary on the practice of fasting in Orthodoxy. His background and vast reading in the Fathers, in critical philosophical methodology, and in the medical sciences have combined to produce a compelling statement about the positive health effects of fasting, its rôle in the maintenance of psychological health, and its crucial rôle in the Orthodox spiritual life. His treatise is scientific, critical, and spiritual at the same time—a rare combination of elements.

Every person in the Orthodox Church should read this short, understandable, and concise statement about fasting. No one can leave this treatise without understanding simply and clearly the wisdom of the Church's teachings about the physical and psychological benefits of fasting and their relationship to the spiritual health that fasting simultaneously facilitates.

Dr. Cavarnos has also published a Greek version of this English text which contains even more materials than the English. For those with abilities in reading the Greek language, this book too may be useful. [Contact the Institute for Byzantine and Modern Greek Studies, 115 Gilbert Rd., Belmont, MA 02478.]

ARCHIMANDRITE AKAKIOS
Center for Traditionalist
Orthodox Studies

2. *HOLINESS: MAN'S SUPREME DESTINY*

Holiness: Man's Supreme Destiny. Belmont, MA: Institute for Byzantine and Modern Greek Studies, 2001. Pp. ix + 96.

Readers who appreciate the erudition and perspicacity that characterize all of Professor Constantine Cavarnos' writings will certainly find the present book, which is a sequel to his earlier and now classic study, *Paths and Means to Holiness* (which Archbishop Chrysostomos and I translated into English, some years ago, and which was published by the Center for Traditionalist Orthodox Studies), equally edifying and instructive. It consists of four excellent lectures, delivered between 1991 and 1997 in a variety of locations in the United States;

namely, "Hunger for Holiness," "Striving for Holiness," "St. Nectarios' Counsels for Spiritual Strivers," and "The Spiritual Strivers' Church in the Home."

The author is to be commended, as always, for making the subtle and profound teachings of the Holy Fathers available to a popular audience. The chapter dealing with St. Nectarios of Aegina is particularly edifying. Based on two of his works, *Thirty-Five Pastoral Epistles* (addressed to the nuns of the Holy Trinity Convent on the island of Aegina, which he himself founded) and *Concerning Care for the Soul,* it demonstrates very clearly that this great luminary of recent times was a wise and compassionate spiritual Father. Faithful to the rich ascetical tradition of the Orthodox Church, and yet also acutely aware of the spiritual debility of modern people, St. Nectarios advised monastics to have recourse to fasting, vigils, and prostrations, but to avoid excesses in so doing. He also emphasized the importance of keeping the body healthy, both by moderate exercise and a good diet.

In the second part of this excellent book, Professor Cavarnos explains how the sublime Patristic precepts that he sets forth in the first three chapters are to be reified in daily life. He points out that Orthodox Christians should not only wear a Cross at all times, but also be careful to make the sign of the Cross with the utmost reverence, and "not hurriedly or mechanically as if we were strumming a guitar or mandolin" (p. 70). He also discusses the important rôle played by Icons, vigil lamps, the prayer rope, incense, and religious books in endowing the Orthodox home with a sacred atmosphere and, thereby, transforming it from a mere dwelling-place into an extension of the Church itself.

The front cover of this fine publication is appropriately adorned with an Icon of the Transfiguration. I heartily recommend it to anyone interested in deepening his or her spiritual life.

BISHOP AUXENTIOS

Center for Traditionalist
Orthodox Studies

3. *MAN'S SPIRITUAL EVOLUTION*

Man's Spiritual Evolution. Belmont, MA: Institute for Byzantine and Modern Greek Studies, 2006. Pp. 95.

In this excellent and beautifully printed sequel to two previous works on the same topic, *Holiness: Man's Supreme Destiny* and *Paths and Means to Holiness,* the latter translated by Archbishop Chrysostomos and Bishop Auxentios and published in English by the Center for Traditionalist Orthodox Studies, Dr. Cavarnos offers a rich and lucid exposition of the ascent, by way of purification and ascetical striving, to spiritual perfection, or deification (Θέωσις), which, as he points out, is nothing other than salvation.

Studded with gems drawn from the abundant storehouse of Patristic wisdom, this short but profound book constitutes a brilliant refutation of the superficial Protestant notion of instant salvation, according to which one has only to "accept Jesus as his personal Lord and Savior" in order to be saved. On the contrary, as the author rightly emphasizes, salvation presupposes a lifelong struggle to cleanse oneself of the passions through prayer, fasting, and inner attentiveness. It is not something that we can achieve by proclamations alone, but entails a total transformation of man and his deification in union with Christ, by Grace, participating in the Perfect Manhood of the Savior, Who, by His Incarnation, wholly transformed our fallen flesh while, at the same time, remaining Perfect God, Who is ineffable, unknowable, beyond all images, and perfectly transcendent.

This new book by Dr. Cavarnos should be required reading for all Orthodox Christians, clergy and laity alike. It will also help the non-Orthodox to grasp better the authentic profundities of the Orthodox Faith, which are so often lost in the frenzy of innovationists and modernists to conform it to the precepts of Western Christianity.

HIEROMONK PATAPIOS

Center for Traditionalist
Orthodox Studies

VIII
LIFE AFTER DEATH

1. *THE FUTURE LIFE ACCORDING TO ORTHODOX TEACHING*

Ἡ Μέλλουσα Ζωὴ Κατὰ τὴν Ὀρθόδοξον Διδασκαλίαν [*The Future Life According to Orthodox Teaching*]. Athens: Ekdoseis "Orthodoxou Typou," 1984. Pp. 79.

This new book by Professor Cavarnos is the outgrowth of a lecture presented to the "St. Andrew New England Greek Orthodox Clergy Brotherhood" several years ago.

Dr. Cavarnos admirably accomplishes the ambitious goal set out in the title of his small volume. In relatively few pages (some 78 pages, including the many footnotes and bibliographical references), he presents the reader with a thorough, well-documented, digestible, and exceptionally reasonable exposition of the Orthodox teaching on the life after death.

The starting point of Cavarnos' study, the "clinically dead" experiences that have proliferated with the improvement of modern medicine, is the same as that found in the late Hieromonk Seraphim's English-language work, *The Soul After Death*—a book, along with selected other volumes of the same author's writings, which Dr. Cavarnos highly recommends to his Greek readers.

Let there be no mistake, however; the present book is not a Greek paraphrase of Father Seraphim's lengthier tome. Cavarnos presents much new material that is more theological in nature, helping the reader to develop a mature mental framework within which to understand better the many experiences known to the Orthodox Fathers in the passage from this life to the next. The main essay in the book is supplemented by six chapters of quotations from all of the important Orthodox sources for this understanding: the Fathers themselves, Scripture, hymnography, etc.

Constantine Cavarnos is renowned for the clear, positive documentation that he offers from Patristic sources, a hallmark of both his spoken and written presentations. From our own reading of the Church Fathers, we are al-

ways struck by the breadth of his knowledge
of Patristic texts, the facility which he seems
to demonstrate in bringing various elements
of the Church's testimony together from scat-
tered sources, and the sharpness with which he
always brings a theological subject into focus.
These traits show Professor Cavarnos to be a
man with astonishing fluency in the theological language of the Church Fathers. His writings are essential for every sober Orthodox
Christian.

Interested readers will be pleased to know
that the Center for Traditionalist Orthodox
Studies will be publishing an English version
of Dr. Cavarnos' book later this year.

HIEROMONK AUXENTIOS
Center for Traditionalist
Orthodox Studies

2. IMMORTALITY OF THE SOUL

Immortality of the Soul. Belmont, MA: Institute
    for Byzantine and Modern Greek Studies,
    1993. Pp. 96.

This book is the most recent of four other major publications by Professor Cavarnos on the general subject of the soul and the after-life: *The Future Life According to Orthodox Teaching, Modern Greek Philosophers on the Human Soul, Plato's View of Man,* and (in Greek) *Symbols and Proofs of Immortality.* The breadth and scope of the book are captured in its subtitle: "The Testimony of the Old and New Testaments, Orthodox Iconography and Hymnography, and the Works of Eastern Fathers and Other Writers of the Orthodox Church." As a work which touches on the most salient Scriptural, iconographic, hymnographical, Patristic, and religious literary traditions of the Orthodox Church, this volume both draws on the conceptual and philosophical foundations of the latter three of the earlier books by Cavarnos that I have listed above, and perfectly complements and amplifies the observations contained in the first book in that list, a volume on the specific teachings of the Orthodox Church on the afterlife. With regard to the iconographic, Patristic, and religious literary witness to the immortality of the soul, the author illustrates the book with Byzantine Icons, analyzes certain ones, and cites the writings of Orthodox Fathers and ecclesiastical authors that span a number of centuries and different national traditions.

Scriptural evidence for the immortality of the soul is, of course, ubiquitous. However, one must approach Biblical data, and especially those of the New Testament, with philological precision, a pursuit for which Dr. Cavarnos, facile in the various forms of the Greek language, is particularly well suited. His treatment is the finest synopsis of this subject that I have ever read. His survey of the depiction of the soul in various Orthodox Icons and hymns is equally excellent, concise, and informative. Of special interest is the author's detailed consideration of the Icon of the Dormition of the *Theotokos*, the symbolism of which is often misinterpreted. Finally, his collection of Patristic accounts of life after death and similar accounts in Orthodox religious literature, ending with the story of the newly-revealed Saints of Lesvos, Raphael, Nicholas, and Irene, constitutes a superb précis of the kinds of spiritual experiences from which the Church's teaching on these matters is ultimately derived.

Dr. Cavarnos' new book is essential reading for thinking, open-minded people who are seeking, not the vindication or validation of their personal opinions and speculation, but the true teachings of the Fathers of the Church.

BISHOP CHRYSOSTOMOS
Center for Traditionalist
Orthodox Studies

IX
MODERN ORTHODOX SAINTS

1. *ST. SAVVAS THE NEW*

St. Savvas the New. Volume 8 in *Modern Orthodox Saints.* Belmont, MA: Institute for Byzantine and Modern Greek Studies, 1985. Pp.
144.

Professor Cavarnos has had a distinguished
career, represented by his writings in classical philosophy, American philosophy, Greek
letters, Byzantine thought, art, theology, Orthodox studies, and Orthodox hagiography.
His works are available in both Greek and
English, in both of which he has fluency and
a charming style and, in translation, in other
languages. His scholarly productivity, from
the Bowen prizes which he won for his philosophical writings while studying at Harvard
to his present study in Orthodox theological
thought, has brought him and his books to the
attention of a wide scholarly readership and
of general readers, too. I mention all of this

so that there is no possibility that one might misunderstand my following comment, to wit, that this author does not receive the attention that he deserves from the scholarly community. However distinguished his career and eminent his position among Orthodox scholars, the fact is that his books call for an acclaim of momentous proportion. But then, again, perhaps this is not best for the man.

If there is a single series in Orthodox hagiography in the English language that one could call indispensable, it is Cavarnos' eight-volume series on contemporary Orthodox Saints, beginning with a volume on Saint Cosmas Aitolos, the "Father" of modern Greek saints. Like their author, these brilliant volumes have received abundant acclaim, critical attention of a positive kind, and enthusiastic praise from the Orthodox faithful. But again, as with the author himself, I do not find the books receiving the attention that should be given to them. Actually, unless one speaks Greek, I do not think that an Orthodox believer in this country can claim any knowledge whatsoever of the modern Greek Church, if these volumes are not on a shelf side-by-side with Holy Scripture, the few Fathers that we have in English, practical spiritual books, and liturgical texts.

In my introduction to *The Ancient Fathers of the Desert* (Holy Cross Orthodox Press, 1980), I pointed out that one must learn of Orthodoxy in a methodical way—a process of learning that is the responsibility of *every* Orthodox Christian. I counted the *Evergetinos*, from which my aphorisms of the desert Fathers are drawn, as one of the basic steps in climbing the spiritual ladder of Orthodox education. Yet, even if I stress the importance of these volumes and dedicate not a little time and effort to their preparation, I must in all truth emphasize that Dr. Cavarnos' series on the modern Greek Saints is an absolute prerequisite for my own volumes. One does not step onto the rung of the ladder until he has first firmly planted his feet on the ground: the Saints of the Church are the very ground in our ascent into Orthodox knowledge.

In the eighth volume of this series, Cavarnos presents us with the life and works of a remarkable and simple holy man of recent times,

Saint Savvas the New, who reposed in 1948 and whose incorrupt and fragrant relics were disinterred as late as 1957. At his repose—something noteworthy for us Old Calendarists—one of the nuns present at his deathbed saw his soul ascend into the heavenly choirs, chanting "in a most sweet voice, 'Announce, O earth, great joy'" (p. 78). It was the eve of the Annunciation of the *Theotokos* by the Julian Calendar, and those churches following the Old Calendar were celebrating this great Feast of the Virgin, whom he so revered. The Saint's repose simply sums up a simple, humble life which was, indeed, a sweet melody among the believers: a life simply, reverently, and piously portrayed by Professor Cavarnos. The works of the Saint—no more than two pages and handwritten—on the correct virtues for a monastic, adorn the book, as though they were an exclamation point to a quiet life that indeed needs to be revealed and loudly proclaimed for the sake of the faithful.

At the end of this handsomely-produced volume, which nicely matches the preceding seven volumes, Cavarnos includes a number of the Icons painted by Saint Savvas. Most are from the island of Kalymnos, where he served as a renowned Confessor, but at least one of them was painted in the convent served by Saint Nectarios on the island of Aegina, where Savvas lived one year with him and spoke of the Saint's sanctity. These Icons, while produced at a time that the Greek and other national Orthodox churches had abandoned the proper Byzantine style for the art of the Italian Renaissance, nonetheless contain a sublime element reminiscent of the Orthodox style. That Professor Cavarnos recognizes this and eloquently comments on it is extremely important. Too often, I am afraid, those who call for a return to the fullness of tradition — and this is a valid call that must be heard — do so in such a way that they deny the action of God's Grace in the Church at all times, and especially at times of apparent decline or deviation from the perfect spiritual standard attained in the Byzantine Church. We see in St. Savvas, a modern Saint, living in modern times, painting in a modern way, the same *inner* depths that we see in our Saints throughout the ages, if simply because God does not abandon those who hold to the Faith. While this cannot justify innovators and individuals who so openly deviate from the standards of Orthodoxy in these days, it is a fact that we must acknowledge, in any stand that we take in the name of the restoration of tradition, that we are surely not really *restoring* tradition, which never dies and is never failing, but simply *restoring* it to its fullness.

Pay attention to the present book and to this series. This is my advice to the reader. I am not, as those familiar with my book reviews know, given much to hyperbole—or at least to positive hyperbole. I am not impressed by scholarship that forgets spirituality. Nor do I think that spirituality is ever genuine unless it is based on thought, study, and reflection. When I recommend the present book, as well as its preceding volumes, then, I do so with great seriousness. This book is indispensable, as are many of Cavarnos' other writings. This is Orthodox scholarship at its best and we should all use it as a model. Though the author is a friend, he is not beyond my criticism. Therefore, I do not praise his work because of our friendship, but I consider him a friend because of his wonderfully beneficial work. I advise readers to make his books their friends.

BISHOP CHRYSOSTOMOS
Center for Traditionalist
Orthodox Studies

2. *ST. METHODIA OF KIMOLOS*

Modern Orthodox Saints, Vol. 9, *St. Methodia of Kimolos.* Belmont, MA: Institute for Byzantine and Modern Greek Studies, 1987. Pp. 123.

Professor Cavarnos' series on modern Greek Saints is by now a classic. Each of the foregoing eight volumes has met with positive critical reviews, and without doubt the present volume will enjoy similar popularity and acclaim. The book has been produced in the format of the other volumes in the series, handsomely and with copious aids to the reader. Not only is the index to Volume Nine complete and useful, but various maps and illustrations help us to know better the milieu in which Saint Methodia struggled and attained to Christian perfection. Particularly helpful is an addendum to Saint Methodia's sayings, which helps us to understand her spiritual advice in terms of related passages from Holy Scripture and from the writings of the Fathers of the Church. This addendum also gives us evidence that this holy woman, as is the case with all Orthodox Saints, taught and guided others according to universal beliefs and precepts shared by all Orthodox teachers across the ages. Dr. Cavarnos' juxtaposition of the Saint's sayings and those of other Orthodox Sages and Saints is a particularly effective way of making this point.

This book contains the life of Saint Methodia, a righteous nun who lived on the island of Kimolos, one of the Cyclades islands, and who reposed in our times (1908). From the biography and *Akolouthia* (or Service) to the Saint composed by the Athonite monk Father Gerasimos Mikragiannanites, a famed Orthodox hymnographer, Cavarnos has presented us in English translation a beautiful commentary on this inspiring holy woman. The biography is translated in its entirety. Many beautiful

excerpts from the *Akolouthia* have been carefully selected and arranged by Dr. Cavarnos
in such a way as to teach us a great deal about
the Saint's life and example. In his introductory
remarks, Cavarnos draws on the recollections
and writings of other sources, producing a
saintly portrait which is well grounded in primary sources and which reflects the consensus
of the secondary materials.

Professor Cavarnos also reproduces in
translation a letter of the saint to her sister,
Anna. This letter gives us clear insight into the
simple, pious spirituality of Saint Methodia.
Everywhere in the letter there is a sense of that
passive and accepting faith that so characterizes our Orthodox saints. The Saint advises her
sister to live her life in preparation for death,
tells her of the miraculous powers of God, and
speaks of no longer "owning" herself, but of
having given her inner self over to the Grace
of God. Oddly enough, at the end of the letter
the Saint advises her sister not to destroy the
letter, but to keep it as a souvenir. So it is that
today we have this beautiful, charming piece

of writing from a contemporary example of the ancient holiness of Orthodox life in Christ.

I have purposely not given details about the life of Saint Methodia in this review. This treasure of details I leave untouched for the reader. It is essential that Orthodox Christians and those who would wish to understand the essence of Orthodox Christianity begin their study of our Faith with readings from the Lives of the Saints. The ascent to Orthodoxy begins on the lowest rung of an intellectual ladder which leads us from the Lives of the Saints to the spiritual counsels of the Fathers (found in the writings of the desert Fathers and the ascetics in the *Evergetinos*) to the final and highest level of intellectual preparation for the spiritual understanding of Orthodoxy, the reading of spiritual theory such as that contained in the *Philokalia* and the theological writings of the great Theologians of the Church. Without having stepped on this first rung, those who move up to the second and third levels of spiritual reading find themselves ill-prepared, standing without firm footing and precariously perched where they are not yet ready to rest. What Dr. Cavarnos has provided in these volumes on modern Orthodox saints is the foundation for all spiritual life.

As I have noted, this book is very handsomely produced. Uncharacteristically—Cavarnos' books are always meticulously prepared and carefully proofread—there are two or three typographical errors in this volume (for example, on p. viii, "send" should read "sent"). These are so few, that I am hard-pressed to note them. However, such instances are, again, so rare in the publications of the Institute for Byzantine and Modern Greek Studies that they seem somehow noteworthy when they do occur. Such notation should not compromise the excellence of this volume and the absolutely essential importance of this book for every Orthodox student and every student of Orthodox Christianity. This book should be on the top of everyone's list of books to buy.

My warmest congratulations to Dr. Cavarnos for another beautiful and profound contribution to Orthodox literature.

BISHOP CHRYSOSTOMOS OF OREOI
Center for Traditionalist
Orthodox Studies

3. BLESSED ELDER PHILOTHEOS (ZERVAKOS)

Blessed Elder Philotheos Zervakos. Volume XI in *Modern Orthodox Saints.* Belmont, MA: Institute for Byzantine and Modern Greek Studies, 1993. Pp. 240.

This eleventh volume of his now famous English-language series on contemporary Orthodox Saints shows the same care and impeccable scholarship that we have learned to expect from the pen of Professor Constantine Cavarnos. It gives us a clear picture of the life, character, thought, miracles, and importance of the Blessed Elder Philotheos (Zervakos) (1884-1980), supplemented, as usual, with hymns appropriate to the liturgical commemoration of this recent Greek Saint.

We should point out, in the way of an incidental explanation, that Dr. Cavarnos refers to this new Greek Saint as "Blessed," "...because it is customary among the Orthodox to use the term 'Blessed' (*Makaristos*) for recently deceased saints who have not yet been officially recognized as saints" (p. xi). He also uses the Saint's last name, a concession, no doubt, to the fact that the use of a family name is common among the Greek clergy of Elder Philotheos' generation, a practice followed by the Elder himself. Strictly speaking, we do not refer to the Church's Saints by their last names, but usually by appellations taken from their place of spiritual struggle (e.g., St. Peter the Athonite), nationality (e.g., St. John the Russian), rank (e.g., St. Elizabeth the Grand Duchess of Russia), etc. (Let us note that examples such as St. Gregory *Palamas* are often used to argue against the Church's strict advocacy of an "impersonal" sanctity that transcends family ties; however, last names, in the time of this and other Saints, were often laudatory or identifying appellations that did not have the significance of "family names" as we understand them today.) Here, in the case of a recently reposed holy man who was widely known by his monastic *and* family name, it seems prudent for the author to have titled his book as he did.

Dr. Cavarnos' excellent portrayal of this modern Greek holy man is enhanced by the fact that he knew the Saint and many of the Saint's contemporaries, friends, and spiritual children. For me personally, this volume of Cavarnos' monumental series is of particular interest. Father Philotheos, himself the spiritual son of St. Nectarios of Aegina, was the spiritual Father of my own spiritual Father, Metropolitan Cyprian of Oropos and Fili. Moreover, I saw the Elder in person some twenty-seven years ago, when I was a student in Greece, and once corresponded with him about Metropolitan Cyprian (before I had met His Eminence), whom the Elder recommended to me as a courageous and holy zealot for his return to the Old Calendar.

The Elder Philotheos' many articles and epistles on spiritual life have been published in Greece, where he is everywhere revered as a Saint. Unfortunately, some of these writings, because of the Elder's strong and uncompromising condemnation of ecumenism and the New Calendar, have been deceptively edited, so as to misrepresent his true views on these matters. His strong condemnations of the *extremist* Old Calendarists (who deny the Orthodoxy of the followers of the calendar innovation), for example, have been intentionally altered to suggest that he condemned the moderate Old Calendarists also, when, in fact, he wholly supported them, following the Old Calendar even within the State Church. When Metropolitan Cyprian was uncanonically deposed by the State Church for returning to the Old Calendar, Father Philotheos wrote that such a deposition logically implied that the New Calendarist Church of Greece should depose all of the Fathers who, in several Church Councils, condemned the New Calendar. These words, too, were deceptively misused by a New Calendarist clergymen who recently charged that they constitute not only a condemnation, but a disavowal, of Metropolitan Cyprian!

The most important thing about Dr. Cavarnos' book is that it provides an *accurate account* of the teachings of Elder Philotheos, containing many selections from his writings and a list of the works which he authored, both published and unpublished. As such, it makes repeated references to his condemnation of ecumenism and his support of the Old Calendarists, thus exposing those who misrepresent the Elder's views on these subjects. With regard to the calendar issue specifically (see esp. pp. 156-163), Cavarnos points out that the Elder considered the adoption of the New Calendar by the Church of Greece a defilement of Church tradition. Œcumenical Patriarch Meletios, who introduced the revised Papal Calendar into the liturgical life of the Greek Church and who died knowing that he had divided Orthodoxy, Father Philotheos characterizes as "censured by his conscience." The introduction of the New Calendar into the Church of Greece the Elder considered uncanonical, unlawful, and the cause of schism. The New Calendarists themselves, he argued, stand condemned before the seventh Œcumenical Synod, three local Councils, and several Church Fathers. Professor Cavarnos is to be commended for setting the record straight in this respect, especially.

I highly recommend this excellent book as one which offers a glimpse into the life of a contemporary Saint who deeply loved the enduring traditions of the Orthodox Church.

BISHOP CHRYSOSTOMOS
Center for Traditionalist
Orthodox Studies

4. *BLESSED ELDER GABRIEL DIONYSIATIS*

Blessed Elder Gabriel Dionysiatis (1886-1983).
Modern Orthodox Saints, Vol. XIII. Belmont,
MA: Institute for Byzantine and Modern
Greek Studies, 1999. Pp. 238.

Dr. Cavarnos has once more put us all in
his debt with this latest volume in the now
classic series, *Modern Orthodox Saints.* Like its
two immediate predecessors, it presents the
life and work of a holy personage not yet officially Glorified by the Church, but honored
by the title "Blessed."

Elder Gabriel, who served for forty years as
Abbot of the Holy Monastery of Dionysiou on
Mount Athos, has been fittingly called "the abbot of abbots of the twentieth century." Three
outstanding traits of this remarkable man
emerge from a reading of this book, which is
the first complete account of him in English: he
was a spiritual Father and guide to hundreds of
people, both monastics and laymen; he was a
staunch upholder of Holy Orthodoxy and traditional monasticism; and he was a veritable

prophet in his denunciations of the social and moral ills of contemporary humanity.

With regard to the second of these traits, Father Gabriel indeed showed himself to be a "new Mark of Ephesus," laying low "the arrogance of the Latinizers," as we read in the beautiful *Kontakion* composed by Dr. Cavarnos specially for this book. In 1964, along with a number of other prominent Athonite Abbots and monks, he issued a sharply-worded *Proclamation* to the Greek people, in which these Confessors warned the Faithful against the unionist activities of the then Œcumenical Patriarch Athenagoras, a pioneer in the move to forge a merely political union between Orthodoxy and the Roman Catholic religion, and those of like mind with him. As late as 1981, when he was totally bedridden, the Blessed Elder still found the strength to expose the anti-Orthodox nature of the official "Dialogue" between Orthodoxy and Roman Catholicism, which had commenced in 1980.

Unfortunately, the anti-ecumenical stand which the Elder embraced on behalf of the Athonite Fathers is now an increasingly rare one. Though, in response to Patriarch Demetrios' ecumenical ventures, as we are told in the present book, the *Synaxis* of the Abbots of the Holy Mountain selected three of the most eminent among them to go to Constantinople, in 1980, to alert the Œcumenical Patriarchate to the perils of such a dialogue (shamefully enough, this committee was not given the opportunity to meet with the Patriarch or his representatives), eleven years later, all of the Athonite Abbots attended the Enthronement of Patriarch Bartholomew, at which Catholics, Protestants and Non-Chalcedonians officially prayed together with the Orthodox. Dr. Cavarnos' volume, then, is a tribute to the ecclesiological sobriety of an Elder whose anti-ecumenical fervor is sadly waning in some circles, but which is a powerful source of inspiration in others.

The author is to be congratulated for including in this volume an excellent article by the Elder Gabriel on the calendar innovation, which was reprinted, by permission, as one of the lead articles in an issue of *Orthodox Tradition*. In his essay, the Elder makes it very clear

that members of the Greek academic community were among those who rose up in protest
against the calendar change in 1924. This is a
very important observation, given the wide-
spread myth that the Greek Old Calendarists
are, at best, poorly educated, and, at worst,
illiterate "half-wits," to use the unfortunate
and ill-advised language of several modernist (New Calendarist) Greek clergy. The Elder
praises the Old Calendarists as *"faithful unto
death with regard to the traditions of the Church"*
and as *"authentic patriots"*—a far cry from the
recent insulting and public characterization of
these faithful Orthodox by Archbishop Stylia-
nos, Exarch of the Œcumenical Patriarchate in
Australia, as a "wretched marginal group."

This outstanding volume is adorned by numerous photographs of the Dionysiou Monastery, where the Elder spent nearly seventy
years of his remarkably long and productive
life, and by reproductions of the title pages of
the ten books that he wrote. We are pleased,
to be sure, that Dr. Cavarnos is planning to
publish another volume in this marvellous series, but rather sad to think that this forthcom-

ing endeavor will constitute the final volume therein. I must, nonetheless, express both my profound gratitude, as well as that of an entire generation of Orthodox in the West, to this indefatigable author for his lasting contributions to the field of hagiography.

HIEROMONK PATAPIOS

Center for Traditionalist
Orthodox Studies

5. *BLESSED ELDER IAKOVOS OF EPIROS, ELDER JOSEPH THE HESYCHAST, AND MOTHER STAVRITSA THE MISSIONARY*

Blessed Elder Iakovos of Epiros, Elder Joseph the Hesychast, and Mother Stavritsa the Missionary. *Modern Orthodox Saints*, Vol. XIV. Belmont, MA: Institute for Byzantine and Modern Greek Studies, 2000. Pp. 156.

In a review of the previous volume of this famous series on Orthodox hagiography, I noted, with considerable regret, that Volume XIV, the volume under review here, was to be the last in the series. This regrettable eventuality is, unfortunately, confirmed by the author in the epilogue to the present book. I offered such comments, not in order to criticize Dr. Cavarnos—far from it—but in order to express my profoundest gratitude to this veritable dean of contemporary Orthodox scholars for his untiring efforts in making some of the outstanding spiritual personalities of the Orthodox Church in recent centuries better known to a wider audience, both Orthodox and non-Orthodox. Thirty years ago, in 1971, the first volume in this series on contemporary Saints, dedicated to St. Cosmas Aitolos, saw the light of publication, and ever since then, English-speaking Orthodox Christians have been slaking their spiritual thirst at this ever-flowing fountain of edification and instruction. In spite of my sense of disappointment, though, I find great consolation in the author's final comments, to the effect that he feels a need to devote his time and energy to other important literary projects. Like the many other admirers of Dr. Cavarnos' work, I hope that these projects will soon come to fruition.

Elder Iakovos (1870-1961), the first subject of this book, was an Athonite Hieromonk. He was moved to compassion by the plight of his countrymen in Epiros, who, some eighty years after the liberation of Greece from the Ottoman Yoke, faced relentless pressure from the Turko-Albanian majority in their homeland to abandon their ancestral Orthodox Faith and become Moslems. Like St. Cosmas Aitolos before him, Father Iakovos was given a blessing to serve the Church in this part of Greece. Among other significant accomplishments, he Liturgized nearly every day for sixty years, and, in a region where spiritual Fathers were few and far between, did much to enhance, among the Faithful, an awareness of the importance of the Mystery of Confession. That his labors were pleasing to God is illustrated by the following facts: on two occasions he was miraculously saved from execution at the hands of the Moslem authorities, and, during the civil war which plagued Greece in the late 1940s, he stepped on a land mine without suffering any bodily harm whatsoever.

A younger contemporary of Elder Iakovos, Elder Joseph the Hesychast of New Skete (1894-1959), has become widely known in recent years, largely through the efforts of Dr. Cavarnos himself, as, for example, in his classic account of the Holy Mountain, *Anchored in God* (first published in 1959). This humble Elder was a spiritual Father to countless individuals, both monastics and lay people, for more than three decades. As an ardent practitioner of the Jesus Prayer, he helped to keep alive the Hesychastic tradition of Mount Athos. Interestingly enough, although his community did not follow a cœnobitic *Typikon*, Elder Joseph made a tremendously important contribution to the restoration of cœnobitic monasticism on the Holy Mountain through his disciple, Elder Ephraim. It was under the latter's Abbotcy, as Dr. Cavarnos observes, that the Monastery of Philotheou, which had, like a number of other Athonite monasteries, been in a state of decline for many years, experienced an unprecedented renewal.

It is gratifying to see mention of Mother Vryenni, the niece of Elder Joseph, and of her brother, the theologian and religious writer Dionysios Batistatos, as examples of people influenced by the Elder's life and teachings. Both of them, we might note, were staunch adherents of the Old Calendar movement who, later in life, embraced the moderate ecclesiology of the Synod in Resistance under Metropolitan Cyprian, Mother Vryenni as Abbess of one of our convents.

The final figure in this collection is Mother Stavritsa Zachariou (1916-2000). She was not, despite her title, a nun, although at one time she seriously considered entering a convent. The appellation "Mother" was, in her case, honorific and a reflection of the tremendous esteem in which she was held by the newly-illumined Orthodox flocks in Kenya, Uganda, and Congo (formerly Zaire). In her early fifties, in response to a vision of Christ Himself, she forsook a comfortable life in America in order to undertake missionary work in East Africa. For nearly thirty years she labored tirelessly in building churches—no fewer than nineteen—and providing them with the necessary interior furnishings. A talented iconographer, she painted numerous Icons in the traditional Byzantine style for these new churches.

I unreservedly recommend this final volume in the series *Modern Orthodox Saints.* Beautifully illustrated, it also features an *Apolytikion* in both Greek and English to each of the three saintly personages whose lives and work are so movingly recounted.

HIEROMONK PATAPIOS

Center for Traditionalist
Orthodox Studies

6. *SAINT ATHANASIOS PARIOS*

Saint Athanasios Parios. Vol. XV in *Modern Orthodox Saints*. Belmont, MA: Institute for Byzantine and Modern Greek Studies, 2006. Pp. 170.

Dr. Cavarnos is to be congratulated for bringing his sterling series of contemporary Saints' lives—a veritable classic of contemporary Orthodox literature—to such a resoundingly successful conclusion. This is, to the best of my knowledge, the first and only full-length book in English on St. Athanasios of Paros (1722-1813), a pivotal, but sadly neglected figure in the *Kollyvades* movement and an outstanding *"Διδάσκαλος τοῦ Γένους"* (Teacher of the [Greek] Nation). It is noteworthy that he was officially Glorified by both the Œcumenical Patriarchate and the (New Calendar) Church of Greece in 1995. One can only wonder, given his adherence to strict interpretations of Church teaching, what he would have to say, were he to come back to life, about the dogmatic deviations and ecumenical excesses of these two Churches in our own day.

A man of phenomenal and broad erudition, characterized, as I have said, by unwavering dedication to Holy Tradition in all its fullness, St. Athanasios wrote many authoritative treatises on Orthodox dogma, apologetics, rhetoric, grammar, and metaphysics. He was also a gifted hymnographer and hagiologist. Unfortunately, with but three exceptions, none of these works has been reprinted in recent times. It is to be hoped that his *Epitome, or Collection of the Divine Doctrines of the Faith*, in particular, will sometime be made available to modern readers.

Like all of its companion volumes, this superb account of the life and work of St. Athanasios offers incontrovertible proof of the perennial spiritual vitality of Orthodoxy, which produces Saints in and for every age.

HIEROMONK PATAPIOS

Center for Traditionalist
Orthodox Studies

X
ECUMENISM AND MODERNISM

1. ORTHODOX TRADITION AND THE MODERN WORLD

Ἡ Ὀρθόδοξος Παράδοσις καὶ ὁ Συγχρονισμός. Athens: "Orthodoxos Typos" Publications, 1971. Pp. 50 + Epilogue.

This small book, *Orthodox Tradition and the Modern World,* is a treasure to be enjoyed by all sober Orthodox. First given as a lecture before the Panhellenic Orthodox Union in Athens in 1970, this work is not for the Orthodox modernist. For those who would say, "Well, Holy Canons are outdated and apply to times past, containing rules that do not hold in our times," or "Do you think that the hair, beard, and cassock make the Priest?"—for those who reduce the mystery of Tradition to such levels of simple-minded prattle or who fail to understand the mystical nexus between what is "external" and what is "internal," this book will be useless. To those who can lift up their thoughts philosophically and theologically to understand that Orthodox tradition is a magnificent blending of time and timelessness, of the fleeting and the eternal, and of the external and internal, this book will be an adventure in reading. It is a book rich in Patristic references, replete with practical insights into Orthodoxy as it meets so-called modernity, and adorned with the pious sentiments of an author who obviously understands Orthodoxy at the profoundest level.

The title of this book in Greek, which cannot be adequately rendered in English, actually refers to Orthodox tradition and how it fits into our times. Dr. Cavarnos very convincingly shows us that an Orthodoxy which accommodates its theology, Iconography, and even the dress which it assigns to clerics to the whims of the world is not a *true* Orthodoxy. It is not an Orthodoxy which acts on its times, but which is conquered by its times. Holy Tradition, an unchanging criterion *within* the world, is ever new and ever transforms the societies in which it is preserved and expressed. I know of no book which better articulates and expresses

Holy Tradition than Dr. Cavarnos' present little work. It is only a pity that the book has not appeared in English, though in our times, when innovators have so eroded the Church's traditions, such a book can be comprehended by most Christians only with great difficulty.

ARCHIMANDRITE CHRYSOSTOMOS
Center for Traditionalist
Orthodox Studies

2. *ECUMENISM EXAMINED*

Ecumenism Examined. Belmont, MA: Institute for Byzantine and Modern Greek Studies, 1996. Pp. 61 + Index.

The subtitle of this book, "A Concise Analytical Discussion of the Contemporary Ecumenical Movement," tells us all that we need to know about its contents. As we would expect from Professor Cavarnos, a distinguished scholar and gifted writer, he develops his theme with precision, leaving the reader with a clear understanding of why ecumenism and Orthodoxy are incompatible. He tells us what ecumenism is, in its various manifestations, why it has been opposed by significant Orthodox spiritual leaders, and describes its divisive effects on the Orthodox Church. This is all done with charity, without polemics, objectively, and with a cutting analysis of the presuppositions of ecumenism that is rare. At the same time, the book is written with a spirit of piety that leaves one with no doubts about the author's personal commitment to the defense of the Orthodox Faith against this pernicious heresy of our age. Those unenlightened about ecumenism will be changed by this book. Anti-ecumenists will find it inspiring. It is destined to be, I believe, *the* book about ecumenism for English-speaking Orthodox at this time.

ARCHBISHOP CHRYSOSTOMOS
Center for Traditionalist
Orthodox Studies

3. *VICTORIES OF ORTHODOXY*

Victories of Orthodoxy. Belmont, MA: Institute for Byzantine and Modern Greek Studies, 1997. Pp. 106 + Index.

Ecumenism and Modernism

It was with great delight that I recently received a hardbound copy—an inscribed gift from the author—of one of Constantine Cavarnos' latest books, *Victories of Orthodoxy*. This excellent volume, consistent in quality with the other writings of this erudite, well-known, and prolific Orthodox writer, is comprised of a collection of homilies and lectures delivered by Dr. Cavarnos on Iconoclasm, the Palamite Controversy, the False Union of Florence, Ecumenism, and the related topic of the Calendar Reform. The central theme of the book is the enduring witness of Orthodox tradition and its consistent victory, in the course of time and trials, over innovation and influences foreign to the ethos of the Church. Thus, the author sketches for us the triumph of the Church's traditional veneration of Sacred Images over the fundamentalistic deviations of the Iconoclasts; the ascendency of the traditional mystical teachings of the Church, as they were taught and practiced by the great Hesychast Father, St. Gregory Palamas, over theological deviations that entered Orthodox spirituality largely from the West; and the rejection of the

143

false union reached, by way of political and theological compromise, between the Orthodox and Papists in the fifteenth century in Florence. He goes on to show that, in our own time, the Orthodox Church is engaged in new struggles against what is foreign and detrimental to Her spirit; that is, in a strong resistance to the *erosion of Her liturgical traditions* (something especially evident in the restoration of Byzantine music and Iconography to Church life); to *the perilous heresy of heresies, ecumenism* (which constitutes a virtual betrayal of the historical and ecclesiological primacy of our Orthodox Faith); and to the *reform of the Church's Festal Calendar,* which has led not only to separation and discord, but which was prompted by ecumenical concerns alien to the spirit of Orthodoxy.

This book is inspirational at several levels. First, it is instructive and easy to read, contributing thereby to an understanding of a number of subjects essential to our Faith. It inspires interest in the Church. Second, it is written with a peaceful spirit, despite its uncompromising message about the unacceptability of current innovations in the Church (organs, Western

music, the Gregorian Calendar, etc.), carefully
setting forth arguments in such a way as to
avoid unnecessary controversy and any kind
of hyperbole. Dr. Cavarnos addresses a wide
audience, preserves a vision—even in his protest against the deviations of innovators in
the Church, today, from the criterion of our
Faith—of the *oneness of Orthodoxy,* and sees
the victory of traditionalism with a clarity that
rises above the temporary separations and fac-
tionalization that so sadly blacken the contemporary traditionalist movement. The loftiness
of his vision inspires hope in the face of the
darkness of these unpleasant manifestations,
fed as they are by petty personal rivalry and
ecclesiastical politics. Finally, in a very subtle
way, by forming our thinking—and this in the
very title of his book—about the subjects which
he discusses, Dr. Cavarnos inspires in us a *hope
for the future* that rises from what he has written
about the past.

It is, of course, obvious that ecumenism and
the calendar reform are still with us, wound-
ing the unity and the integrity of Orthodoxy.
They have been, and still are, the cause of great

temptation for the Faithful. The national Orthodox Churches are literally beset by political ecumenism, and those of us resisting this evil force are constantly besieged by the relentless counter-reaction of the ecumenical power-structure. But Professor Cavarnos nonetheless gives us hope that these new enemies of Orthodoxy will one day be overcome, as were Her past enemies, so that new victories can be remembered and commemorated among the Orthodox Faithful in the years ahead. He reminds us that *Orthodoxy is always triumphant* and that, just as the perils of the past were overcome by faithful and dedicated resistance, so the dangers of the present will one day fade away with the *victory of Holy Tradition.*

This book is handsomely printed, beautifully bound, extremely well-written, and something that every sober resister should read and pass on to all Orthodox Christians who pine for the beauty of our Faith in its wholeness, as it is realized in the fullness of Holy Tradition, and who see the dangers that threaten that wholeness in our hapless days. This volume illuminates the past, affords critical insight into the present, and gives us hope for the future—no small accomplishment.

ARCHBISHOP CHRYSOSTOMOS
Center for Traditionalist
Orthodox Studies

XI

ECCLESIASTICAL ARTS

1. *BYZANTINE CHURCHES OF THESSALONIKI*

Byzantine Churches of Thessaloniki. Belmont, MA: Institute for Byzantine and Modern Greek Studies, 1995. Pp. 78 + Appendix, Bibliography, and Index.

The primary ancestral city of the Greek part of my family is Thessaloniki, *the center of Greek Macedonian culture.* I am thus naturally attracted to this book, which describes and recounts the history of seven of that city's oldest and most beautiful Churches. Thessaloniki, built on the ruins of the ancient city of Thermi, was rebuilt in 316 B.C. and named after the sister of Alexander the Great. In 1984, it celebrated two thousand three hundred years of continuous existence. Among its claims to social and cultural eminence are its Byzantine Churches—some built in the early Christian centuries—which Photios Kontoglou considered the finest extant monuments of Byzantine art.

Ecclesiastical Arts

Dr. Cavarnos' new book, further evidence of his astonishingly prolific scholarly output, contains a Foreword by Sophia Ahtarides, a graduate of the University of Thessaloniki and an accomplished student of things Byzantine. A Greek text of her useful introductory remarks appears at the back of the book. The text proper of this volume is a very sensitive and insightful description of the architecture and decoration of the Churches in question, demonstrating not only a keen understanding of aesthetic principles, but deep spiritual discernment. Having seen most of the Churches described, I can attest to the precision and detail with which each is considered.

I would recommend this treasure to anyone who loves Byzantine architecture, the classical spiritual arts of the Orthodox Church, and the Saints of our Church, about whom much is said in this book, by virtue of the various Saints to which the several Churches are dedicated.

ARCHBISHOP CHRYSOSTOMOS
Center for Traditionalist
Orthodox Studies

2. *BYZANTINE CHANT*

Byzantine Chant. Belmont, MA: Institute for Byzantine and Modern Greek Studies, 1998. Pp. 102.

Dr. Constantine Cavarnos enjoys the well-deserved reputation of a scholar who is always able to present a subject with that crafted balance of succinctness and clarity which engages a reader yet never tires him. This finely-honed ability, the envy of any author, manifests itself throughout his impressive works, a body of writings astonishing in their extensiveness and erudition. This talent Dr. Cavarnos has once again applied to great effect in this latest of his books, which our monastery received with immense pleasure as a gift from the author.

This book is an accessible introduction to the essential features of Byzantine chant, that peak expression of Orthodox Christian hymnody. Pithily defining this "purely vocal music" as "cadenced poetic prose," the author briefly describes its characteristic components of monophony, antiphony, *isocrátema, can-*

onárchema, modes, tempo, notation, *prólogoi, prosómoia,* and style. A helpful feature is the inclusion of examples of the fifteen most commonly encountered *prólogoi,* the archetypal musical patterns of Orthodox hymnography, written in the distinctive notation unique to Byzantine chant.

In detailing these technical aspects, Dr. Cavarnos does not fail to emphasize that Byzantine chant ultimately serves as an aural vehicle for spiritual content. Thus, his technical treatment of Byzantine music also introduces us to profound theological ideas and matters of spiritual loftiness.

We heartily recommend this text to all who wish to understand and to appreciate the unquestioned merits of Byzantine chant as the musical and theological medium *par excellence* of the Divine Services.

HIEROMONK GREGORY

Center for Traditionalist
Orthodox Studies

3. *GUIDE TO BYZANTINE ICONOGRAPHY*

Guide to Byzantine Iconography: Volume Two.
Boston, MA: Holy Transfiguration Monastery, 2001. Pp. 160.

The first volume of this scholarly endeavor
was hailed by one reviewer as "among the very
best and most authoritative works on the subject of Byzantine iconography." In my estimation, the present volume more than lives up
to the high reputation deservedly enjoyed by
its predecessor. Beautifully printed and lav-
ishly illustrated with Icons from Mount Athos,
Constantinople, Greece, Serbia, Sicily, Georgia,
and Russia, it encompasses, in the first chapter,
such festal Icons as those depicting the Wash-
ing of the Disciples' Feet, the Mystical Supper,
Christ Healing the Paralytic, the Nativity of the
Theotokos, the Elevation of the Precious Cross,
and the Entry of the *Theotokos* into the Temple;
and, in the ensuing chapters, the Holy Trinity,
the *Theotokos*, St. John the Forerunner, and the
Holy Angels. In a short appendix, Professor
Cavarnos summarizes the views of St. Nec-

tarios and Photios Kontoglou on the nature of archetypes in iconography.

Throughout the book, the author quotes the Gospel passages on which the various Icons are based and supplements these with well-chosen hymnographic texts. He explains the significance of each scene with characteristic lucidity and attention to detail. There are so many illuminating comments in this work that I cannot possibly discuss them all. I will simply mention four points on which Dr. Cavarnos offers particularly valuable insights.

First, he rightly observes that the Greek inscription "Ὁ Μυστικὸς Δεῖπνος" is quite incorrectly translated as "The Last Supper," not only by Western writers, but also, unfortunately, by many Orthodox, who ought to know better. The adjective "last" has absolutely nothing to do with the inner, spiritual meaning of this event. Cavarnos points out that, if anything, it should be called "The Perpetual Supper," because, "as a mystical event the 'Supper' takes place at every Divine Liturgy" (p. 29).

Secondly, Professor Cavarnos highlights the great importance of the scene recounted by St. Luke, in which Christ breaks bread at Emmaus in the presence of the Holy Apostles Luke and Cleopas. The relative rarity of this depiction in Orthodox churches is somewhat surprising, given that the Gospel appointed for the Divine Liturgy on Bright Tuesday is precisely this pericope from St. Luke, whereas for the remainder of Bright Week—and indeed, up until Pentecost—almost all of the readings are taken from St. John's Gospel. Perhaps, as the author conjectures, this is simply a matter of limited space or of missing the significance of the event as an empirical verification of the Resurrection. In any case, given its obvious Eucharistic ramifications, it would certainly be desirable if this pivotal scene were to be included in the mural decoration of churches.

Thirdly, Dr. Cavarnos emphasizes that the Icon known as "The Hospitality of Abraham," which portrays the three Angels who appeared to Abraham at the Oak of Mamre, should always include the figures of Abraham and Sarah and should be entitled "The Hospitality of Abraham" and not "The Holy Trinity." Without Abraham and Sarah, the historical dimension of this theophany is obscured and the impression is all too easily conveyed that the Angels somehow represent the Divine nature, whereas, according to the hymnography of the Church, what Abraham saw was a vision of God and a foreshadowing (τύπος) of the Incarnation.

Fourthly, with regard to the iconic figure known as "The Ancient of Days," the author maintains, as do the Holy Fathers, that this is Christ, and not God the Father. The proper way to represent the First Person of the Trinity is as a hand emerging from Heaven and bestowing a blessing. However, although this image of the Ancient of Days is perfectly in accordance with Orthodox Christology, Professor Cavarnos recommends that it not be used in the adornment of churches, on the grounds that it tends to mislead those less educated in theology into supposing that it does, in fact, represent God the Father.

The author tells us in the preface to his present work that a third volume will be needed to complete this magnificent contribution to the study of Byzantine iconography. Let us hope that, amid all of his other important publishing projects, Dr. Cavarnos will soon find the time to finish work on a final volume in his series on iconography. We are all indebted to him for the years of painstaking research that have borne such rich fruits in the two volumes that have appeared so far. The *Guide to Byzantine Iconography* is destined, I believe, to become a classic treatment of this fascinating and crucial subject.

Hieromonk Patapios

Center for Traditionalist
Orthodox Studies

4. *BYZANTINE CHURCH ARCHITECTURE*

Byzantine Church Architecture. Belmont, MA: Institute for Byzantine and Modern Greek Studies, 2007. Pp. 61 + Bibliography and Index.

This latest book by Professor Constantine Cavarnos, the Harvard-educated President of the Institute for Byzantine and Modern Greek Studies, is a masterpiece of clear writing and one of the finest summaries of Byzantine architecture—replete with rich and learned references to Byzantine aesthetic principles in general—available today. Dr. Cavarnos is the author of more than a dozen books on Byzantine art and architecture, Iconography, classical aesthetics, and almost every aspect of the Orthodox spiritual life, comprising less than a quarter of his published volumes. As a philosopher and one of the more eminent scholars of the contemporary Orthodox Church, he continues to produce scholarship, even as an octogenarian, that is inevitably received *cum laude magna*. This excellent treatise will be no exception to this rule, I am sure; it is scholarship *comme il faut*.

Byzantine Church Architecture is comprised of four short chapters, the first being a concise introduction to Byzantine architecture, defining its purpose and scope, presenting some of the essential nomenclature in the field, and illustrating all of this material with descriptions of extant Byzantine Churches (the majority from the ancient city of Thessaloniki). There follow three chapters which present and analyze particular examples of Byzantine

157

architecture, two of them (Chapters Two and Four) dedicated to the famous Church of Hagia Sophia in Constantinople and various Byzantine Churches throughout Greece, and a third (Chapter Three) featuring a brilliant criticism of Frank Lloyd Wright's failed attempt at Byzantine architecture at the New Calendarist Annunciation Greek Orthodox Church in Milwaukee, Wisconsin. Stating his well-known and commendable "distaste for controversy," but expressing his concern for the "future of Greek Orthodoxy in America" (p. 37), Cavarnos objectively, carefully, and definitively establishes why this Church "is not at all appropriate to Eastern Orthodox Christianity, is not in accord with the needs of Orthodox worship," and violates Wright's own principle of form following function, "[t]hat is, the purpose for which a building is constructed should determine its form" (p. 43).

The foregoing chapters are followed by two appendices, both by the celebrated Greek iconographer and spiritual writer, Photios Kontoglou: Appendix A, containing his comments on the famous Rotunda Church of St. George in Thessaloniki (originally a mausoleum, constructed in 319 A.D.), which Professor Cavarnos also discusses in Chapter One; and Appendix B, which is an anthology of insightful comments by Kontoglou on Byzantine architecture in general. The book also includes a short but very useful bibliography, containing works in both Greek and English, some of Cavarnos' own masterful volumes featured among the latter. There are two good indices, one of proper names cited in the book, the other of subjects covered in the book.

This is a book which can be beneficially read by anyone. It demands no expertise or background in architecture, aesthetics, or theology, and it is simply but elegantly written. It is also a book which every Orthodox Christian and those with passing or extended interest in Orthodox Church architecture, art, and adornment should read and study with care. It is a virtual primer in Orthodox Church "form" and "function."

ARCHBISHOP CHRYSOSTOMOS
Center for Traditionalist
Orthodox Studies

INDEX OF PROPER NAMES

160

Index of Proper Names

Iakovos of Epiros, Elder, 131, 133-134

John Chrysostomos, St., 15, 61
Joseph the Hesychast, Elder, 131, 134

Kallistos of Diokleia, Metropolitan, 28
Kontoglou, Photios, 78-96, 148, 153, 158-159

Lamarck, Jean Baptiste, 39-42

Mark of Ephesos, St., 31-32, 128
Methodia of Kimolos, St., 117-120

Nectarios of Aegina, St., 50, 53, 61, 80, 101, 115, 124, 152
Nicodemos the Hagiorite, St., 10, 27, 29, 61, 70-71

Patapios Agiogregorites, Hieromonk, xi, 8
Philotheos of Longovarda, Archimandrite, 79-80, 122-126
Photios the Great, St., ix, 1, 7, 24-25, 61
Plato, 37, 50, 62, 66, 70, 73
Plutarch, 54-56
Pythagoras, 44-48

Savvas the New, St., 111, 114-115
Socrates, 37, 50

INDEX OF SUBJECTS

Index of Subjects

Philokalia, 11, 15, 26-30, 120
philosophy, 16-19, 60-63
phyletism, 71, 75
Pre-Socratics, 49, 73

Seven Sages, the, 49-53
spiritual evolution, 103
Stoicism, 61-62

terminology, 14-15, 17, 20, 46, 61
theology, 3, 5, 12, 17, 26, 60, 62, 71-72, 76, 84-85, 97,
 111, 140, 155, 159
therapy, 44, 48, 54

wellness, 54-56